WOMEN'S VOICES IN
MIDDLE EAST MUSEUMS

Gender, Culture, and Politics in the Middle East

Leila Ahmed, Miriam Cooke, Simona Sharoni, *and* Suad Joseph
Series Editors

Other titles in Gender, Culture, and Politics in the Middle East

WOMEN'S VOICES *in* MIDDLE EAST MUSEUMS

CASE STUDIES IN JORDAN

CAROL MALT

Syracuse University Press

Syracuse University Press
Syracuse, New York 13244-5160
Copyright © 2005 by Carol Malt

First Edition 2005

05 06 07 08 09 10   6 5 4 3 2 1

The paper used in this publication meets the minimum requirements of
American National Standard for Information Sciences—Permanence of
Paper for Printed Library Materials, ANSI Z39.48–1984.∞™

Library of Congress Cataloging-in-Publication Data
Malt, Carol.
   Women's voices in Middle East museums : case studies in Jordan /
Carol Malt.— 1st ed.
      p. cm.— (Gender, culture, and politics in the Middle East)
   Includes bibliographical references and index.
   ISBN 0-8156-3078-6 (cloth : alk. paper)
   1. Museums—Arab countries—History.   2. Museums—Jordan—
History.   3.   Women—Arab countries—History.
4. Muslim women—Arab countries—History.   5. Civilization, Arab.
6. Arab countries—Intellectual life.   I. Title.   II. Series.
AM79.4.M35 2004
069'.082'095695—dc22   2004021014

Manufactured in the United States of America

Contents

Carol Malt received her doctorate from the University of Miami. She is an independent scholar who has been the executive director of three art museums and has curated many exhibitions. She is a museologist specializing in museums of the Middle East and women's empowerment in the Middle East and North African (MENA) countries. She has written extensively about art and museums for various journals and is the author of the historical biography *The Free Woman*. She has received several awards and fellowships, including two Fulbright Senior Scholar grants (Jordan 1999 and Morocco 2004) and a Palestinian American Research Center fellowship (2001). She teaches a course on women in the Muslim world at the University of West Florida.

Preface

In 1998, I received a Fulbright Senior Scholar grant to conduct research on the museums of the Middle East and the women who founded or work in them. I wanted to know how museums represent, serve, empower, and advance society in general and women in particular. For the purpose of this research, the term *Middle East* was inclusive of Egypt, Iraq, Jordan, Lebanon, the West Bank of Palestine, Syria, and Turkey. Jordan was used as a case study for discussion.

Like other passionate endeavors, my research grew in scope and intensity as I explored the subject. I sought to include information on related topics: the cultural centers, arts organizations, and art galleries interacting with these museums; art education and museological training; and the women arts activists, art educators, and collectors participating in them.

This research was not the kind that had me sitting at the feet of a world-renowned guru, rapt at attention. Nor was it research where I spent hours reading in the libraries, for little material has been published on the subject. I seemed to be creating something new. I hoped to provide historians with information on the development of museums in the Middle East; university museum studies programs with a perspective on the history, issues, and operation of museums in the Middle East; and women's studies programs with relevant information on women in the workforce and their achievements. Live interviews would put faces on my data.

The idea for this project came from a conversation in 1996 with Esin Atil, senior curator of Islamic art at the Freer Gallery of Art. During a meeting of the North American Historians of Islamic Art in Washington, we discussed my interest in Middle East museums. She confronted me with a challenge: "Did you know that there are more women curators working in

Middle East museums than in the museums of Europe and the United States combined?" As an art museum director and former curator myself, I wanted to learn more.

One of my first tasks was to define the word *museum*. My definition and my perception of the word did not always concur with the perceptions of others in the Middle East as to its meanings and connotations. Many there regard *museum* as synonymous with the word *antiquities*, as in this definition from a Jordanian museum curator: "A museum should reflect the old civilizations." When I asked others in the profession the question "What is a museum?" I received such answers as "A museum should recover a sense of belonging to local history and traditions," and "A museum is a place for the old things, for ancient things, things that show us the past and things we don't use anymore." And also, "A museum? It's for the old people." In my definition, a museum had to be four things: nonprofit, educational in purpose, professionally staffed, and opened to the public on some regularly scheduled basis.

As my research progressed, I realized that the diversity found in North American museums did not exist in the same way in the Middle East. Further, some of my training in museology did not, could not, and should not apply there. How dare I say that? The museum boards I have served would stare at me in disbelief. For is there not one professional way to manage a museum, care for collections, educate people, train personnel, and interpret history? That is why we have standards, accreditation, museum assessment programs, and annual meetings.

A particular incident clarified this for me. As I neared the end of my stay in Jordan, I was asked to give a lecture on museums. I chose an olive-colored pantsuit to wear that I had just gotten back from an overly zealous local tailor who had reconstructed the pants that had been two sizes too big for me into something that felt much too tight. As I zipped up, I was reminded of the story of the suit in Hanan Ashrawi's book, *This Side of Peace*. It was an analogy to a peace plan that was stitched together all wrong. She wrote of a man whose tailor kept altering his suit to fit him, and skewed it until it hardly resembled a suit at all—or he a man at all. I also recalled the words of Suha Shoman, the founder of the Darat al Funun, where I was to speak. She told me that the strategies and formal policies of American museums were often unnecessarily rigid and somewhat inappropriate for institutions in Jordan. She believed that it would be wiser for Jordan's museums to develop their own policies, based on and inspired by other professionally run museums but modified to suit the realities there.

My interest in the Middle East began as a young visitor to museums, expanded with residency in Palestine, then formal university education in the United States. My interest in gender issues and women's participation in Middle Eastern society was explored on many levels over time. As noted by Claudine Brown in her foreword to *Gender Perspectives* (Glaser and Zenetou 1994), a pattern of male leadership in American museums was evident in the 1970s, when I entered the museum profession. It reflected the male leadership patterns of the society in which I grew up. And, like Brown, I was so pleased with my work, so fulfilled by my career, that I took little notice of the women's movement or the dynamics of women's status in the workplace at the time. Over time, however, my awareness of gender bias grew, particularly after I had achieved advanced degrees and professional experience. With this background and interest, I felt it useful to explore the universality of women's issues in the museum profession.

Encouraged by Flora Kaplan's *Museums and the Making of "Ourselves"* (1994), in which she points out that museums themselves are worthy of study as social institutions, I broadened my research to include not only the history of museums, their collections, exhibitions, and purpose, but also how they function and what was important enough to be "enshrined" in them. In my case studies, my intent was not to list and compare cultural or physical parity between American museums and their Middle Eastern counterparts. However, it became apparent that many of the issues I was investigating were indeed analogous.

To gather my data, I used several investigative methods: active tours of sites, interviews with personnel, passive reference and literary search, and the structured format of questionnaires.

General publications provided useful, though limited, documentary material on the major museums of Egypt, Lebanon, Iraq, Syria, and Turkey, but little historical or museological information was available on Jordan and the West Bank of Palestine; I obtained primary source information for case studies on the types, locations, facilities, and programs of museums throughout Jordan and the West Bank from site visits. Although I list museum institutions and collections in the Gaza Strip in appendix A, I did not actively conduct research there, and more detailed analysis awaits a future visit. When I visited individual sites, I photographed each museum's façade and portions of the interiors. If the curator or administrator was a woman, I interviewed her and photographed her behind her desk in her office. No one refused my request. With the permission of the interviewed person, tape recordings were also made of the interviews.

This book begins with an introduction that places Middle Eastern museums in historical context. Then follows a cultural overview of women in Middle Eastern society, referencing historical precedents in the Middle East and focusing particularly on women in Jordan. I then discuss women and museum work. This is followed by case studies of Jordanian women within the museum arena. For these case studies, I interviewed twenty-four women founders, curators, and administrators in museums. In addition, I met with eighteen women collectors, arts activists, and art educators. Some of the questions I asked were: Why did women choose museum work? How did they get there? What did their husbands or families think of this work? What were their goals, aspirations, accomplishments, and problems? I heard many speak of inequality and of the difficulties of balancing both a career and a family. I also heard, over and over, of their need for help in museological training. They needed books and practical advice. They wanted, and welcomed, people to come and sit with them, walk around their exhibits, and discuss the displays—and many lacked the technology of computers and software for collections management. Although sometimes frustrated, they were pleased with their careers, and proud.

At the conclusion of the interviews, opportunities arose for more personal conversation and revelations. Beyond their professional abilities, some of these founders, curators, and artists revealed eccentric tastes and unusual interests. One was reported to love a spoonful of honey every morning—so much so that she carried honey with her whenever she traveled. She also kept an ostrich and a peacock in her garden. One collected stones of interesting shapes; another collected turkey bones to use in her sculptures; one collected miniatures and dollhouses; another made puppets and gave puppet shows in churches. A few collected village costumes and Bedouin jewelry, and many collected art books.

Several aspects of the research should be clarified. Many names of people and sites have varying spellings when translated from Arabic; spellings vary even among official government publications. For site names, I have chosen the spelling most commonly used in English, but I have made reference to some variations. As for individual names and collections within

Jordan, I have whenever possible followed the spellings given in the responses to my questionnaire.

Although I have traveled in, lived in, and written about the Middle East for many years, I have had no training in anthropology and no formal experience in cultural fieldwork. My research and publications have always been in art history or art criticism, or have been museum specific. In conducting this research, I owe much to scholars in anthropology and sociology whose publications laid important groundwork for me to draw upon and who put my concerns into perspective. Their works are listed in the reference section of this book. Some issues were of great concern, notably the dilemma, raised by Erika Friedl (1995) and Rosemary Sayigh (1996), of researchers who invite their subjects to reflect on themselves without taking into account the effect of such intimate confidences on the objectivity of the study. The more I became a friend and colleague to the women I was interviewing, the more I became an actor in their lives and their stories. Lila Abu-Lughod (1986) decribes the asymmetrical relationship that develops during research—asking for honesty but being unwilling to be open about oneself; this became my own dilemma, for I did not share my personal life.

Throughout this research it was the museum women themselves who inspired me. They gave me their time, shared their lives, thoughts, and values, and helped me produce this document, which goes beyond buildings and objects to honor ideas, and lives of perseverance and dedication.

Introduction

Museums in Middle Eastern Society

Museums are the trophies of stability and peace.

—*Suhail Bisharat*

Historical Overview: Egypt, Iraq, Lebanon, Syria, Turkey, and the West Bank of Palestine

Because this research focuses on women who have chosen work in the museum field, it is first necessary to examine Middle Eastern museums themselves, particularly in light of their history and aims. Although the human desire to amass booty and plunder is ancient and universal, museums, as we know them today, are a Western idea. They were conceived as repositories for objects and information that were in some way important or valuable to a community or its power structure.

Archeologists use human-fashioned objects as indicators of civilization. Collecting and displaying items of beauty and cultural identity can enhance a society's prestige and emphasize its continuity; in addition, the presentation of booty from other cultures—particularly the spoils of war or the fruits of foreign trade—underlines a society's international position and reinforces its power roles and dynastic pride. According to Suhail Bisharat, former director of Jordan's National Gallery of Fine Arts, museums in the Middle East "evolved from their original role as forbidden temples, great warehouses to store and protect the rulers' symbols of power" (1994, 159).

These early "symbols of power" were most probably made by and for men. The patriarchal society produced, collected, and honored such trophies as swords, armor, and challenge or game awards. It was not until the late nineteenth century that objects made by and for women began to be publicly collected. They were usually more utilitarian and fragile because they were not made of materials from the traditional trades or guilds reserved for males.

Amassing a collection meant, of course, making a home for it. The tradition of collecting Middle East artifacts from the eastern Mediterranean region began early. Pliny mentions how the Romans appreciated the opulence of the Middle East and that art was collected and publicly displayed before the first century. There was also an active art market. Alexander the Great is said to have sent Aristotle examples of plunder from the lands he conquered. Ptolemy Soter, influenced by the Hellenizing policy of Alexander, founded the museum at Alexandria in Egypt. Although this was essentially a library, it serves to illustrate the important point that libraries contained things we now identify as works of art: illuminated manuscripts, miniature paintings, and drawings.

The collecting of manuscripts and miniature paintings gives validity to the role of libraries as museums in antiquity. Many public and private libraries were established in major Middle Eastern urban centers other than Baghdad, including Damascus, Alexandria, and Cairo; some could be found even in the smaller cities.

The first great library of the Islamic world was established in Baghdad during the early ninth century. Founded either by the Caliph Harun al-Rashid or by the Caliph al-Ma'mun, it was located next to a college, the Dar al-'Ilm, or House of Knowledge/Wisdom. In 1258, when the Mongols destroyed the city of Baghdad, historians listed thirty-six libraries.

Although an early tradition of amassing collections of artistic objects for the benefit of citizens of the state did not exist in the Middle East, important objects and information were collected and preserved and were available for interpretation in the *madrasas* (religious schools) and through the *waqf* system (an Islamic system for making benevolent endowments for religious, educational, or charitable purposes). Rulers often kept royal objects, especially those they inherited, in the treasury *(khazneh)*. Ceremonial, symbolic, artistic, or divine objects were collected and maintained to strengthen power and as an act of reverence rather than for educational purposes or the enlightenment of the citizenry.

In medieval Europe, the churches and monasteries preserved ecclesiastical relics but showed little interest in the collection of manmade objects of aesthetic value, with the exception of illuminated manuscripts, which they kept in their libraries. Monasteries and churches often began collections of old silver and textiles, as well as utilitarian objects having to do with liturgy. In contrast, this type of collecting was unusual in the Muslim Middle East for there were no monasteries and no formal priesthood to act as keepers of the collections. And, although fine carpets were often used in mosques, very few man-made artistic objects were saved or collected that were not functional or architectural in purpose.

The museum as a public institution appeared in Europe in the eighteenth century. These early museums were actually envisioned not as places for the public but as places for the educated or enlightened. The first major museum to be called such was the Ashmolean Museum at Oxford University, founded in 1683 (a smaller university museum was founded in Basel in 1671). It would be almost another one hundred years before other major museums were established in the West: in England, the Royal Academy of Arts in 1768 and the British Museum in 1753; in Madrid, the Museo Nacional de Ciencias Naturales in 1771; in the United States, the Charlestown, South Carolina, Museum in 1773, and, in Paris, the Muséum de la République (now the Musée Nationale du Louvre) in 1793.

The first institutions in the Middle East to be known as museums were established in Ottoman Turkey. An early example is the first Byzantine church in Istanbul, the fourth-century Haghia Eirene. It was later incorporated into the area of the royal palace, where janissaries began to use it as an armory. By the nineteenth century, the accumulation of old weapons inside led to the building becoming the first Turkish military museum. It is known today as the St. Irene Museum. The Archeology Museum in Istanbul was built in the mid-nineteenth century, its curator the European-trained artist and archeologist Osman Hamdi Bey.

Also in Istanbul, the Topkapi Palace, home of Ottoman sultans and the administration center of the Ottoman Empire for four hundred years, originally contained several treasury areas: the relics of the prophet Muhammad, the Ambassadors' Treasure, the Inner Treasury, and the Equestrian Treasury were each separately housed. It is believed that the sultans' treasures were originally kept in the Seven Towers Gate section of the city walls. These treasures of Topkapi were stored in closets and chests until the time of Abdülmecid I, who ordered that some of the artifacts be put on exhibit during the Crimean War (1854–56), and the sultans who followed him continued this practice. After the establishment of the Turkish Republic in 1923, the palace was transformed into a museum. In addition, Kemal Atatürk turned Aya Sofya into a museum in 1936; and in 1937 the Istanbul Museum of Painting and Sculpture was established by his directive at the crown prince's quarters in the Dolmabahçe Palace complex.

In the late nineteenth and early twentieth centuries, museums were established in other countries in the Middle East. Most were founded by men. In 1867 a museum was founded at the American University of Beirut in Lebanon using the Cyprus collection of the American consul, General Cesnolla; the Museum of Egyptian Antiquities in Cairo was built in 1902; Syria's National Museum in Damascus opened in 1919. The Palestine Archeological Museum (Rockefeller Museum), funded by John D. Rockefeller, Jr., in Jerusalem, was completed in 1935 and opened in 1938. Other Jerusalem museums of that time included the Islamic Museum (1923), the Greek Orthodox Patriarchate Museum (1884), and the Franciscan Museum (1902). In Jordan, Emir Abdullah ordered the creation of a museum in Jerash upon his return from a visit to Jerusalem in 1923.

A notable exception to the history of male founders of museums was that of Iraq's National Museum in Baghdad, which was founded by the Englishwoman Gertrude Bell. On October 13, 1923, she wrote to her father: "We are starting what do you think the Iraqi Museum!" (Bell 1927, 543).

Women began to exert significant influence on museum development in the Middle East after 1950. In 1962, when Jordan controlled the West Bank of Palestine, Hind Husseini began collecting costumes and other objects of Palestinian heritage for a folk museum; named the Dar El Tifl El Arabi Institution (the Palestinian Arab Folklore Centre of Dar El Tifl), it was finally established in 1979. Women in other areas likewise recognized the need to collect and preserve cultural artifacts. In 1972, after founding the In'ash El Usra in El Bireh, near Ramallah—an institution designed to shelter, train, and promote women—Sameeha Khalil supported the creation of the Palestinian Folkloric Museum (Museum of Heritage of the Palestine People) in that facility. Also in 1972, Julia Dabdoub and the Arab Women's Union, seeking both to help women economically and to preserve folk heritage, founded the Bethlehem Museum.

Concerning the late development of museums in the Middle East, Henrique Abranches argues that Arabs have been dispossessed of their own artistic creations and their museums do not reflect the greatness of the Arab peoples: "[The Arab's] culture identity is smothered when seeking his own essence and originality, and his identification with his past is blurred by colonialism and lingering colonialist attitudes" (1983, 19–33). Yet it is evident that Jordan, as well as Egypt, Lebanon, Syria, and Iraq, benefited from the expertise of foreign experts in the establishment of their museums. Early on, British archeologists were influential in the planning of museums at historic sites, and the British continued to be a presence in Jordan's archeological programs even after the establishment of the Jordanian kingdom. The Jordanian government realized the importance of its history and used this foreign expertise to properly research and manage its archeological program, both internally and internationally, until it could train its own experts.

However, it was not unusual for museums in the colonial territories to be mere warehouses or to treat the peoples who created the objects housed in museums as unimportant. Reflecting the artificial role they played, colonial museums were often little more than storehouses, and the objects on display lost their meaning, spirit, and context or were interpreted in light of the interests of those in control. "As such," Abranches argues, "the Colonial museum bore no relation to its indigenous surroundings, to the extent that it completely ignored its existence" (1983, 21–22).

This colonial period in the Middle East empowered a political and societal relationship that was unequal; its assumptions and perceptions, based on inequitable power relationships, encouraged stereotypes of inferiority and fantasy. Beginning in the nineteenth century, this European fascination with the Middle East was manifested visually through the Orientalist school of painting and also influenced poetry, prose and the performing arts. It imposed on the population a stigma of inferiority in cultural expression that is still at issue. Even today, museums often perpetuate this issue of inferiority. As Porterfield explains, "Since their invention two centuries ago, museums and galleries in Europe and the United States have presented little in the way of works by contemporary Arab women artists, yet they have purveyed a great deal of Orientalism, art by Westerners (usually men) about the East." Moreover, "until very recently, Western audiences viewed Orientalist pictures as authentic representations by the artist of his Eastern subjects" (1994, 59).

Historically, private collections existed in the Middle East, and they do so today. Many farsighted patrons began private collections in the early twentieth century, wishing to see their national heritage preserved. Two such collections that became museums in Cairo are Mahmoud Khalil's museum and Major Gayer-Anderson's Bayt al Kiritliya. The Nicholas Ibrahim Sursock Museum, founded in 1952 in Beirut as an exhibit and conference center, claims to be the only modern-art museum in Lebanon. Sursock bequeathed his personal estate and real estate to the municipality. In addition to its collections of Islamic ceramic ware, Greek icons, rare books, and contemporary Lebanese painting, the museum presents exhibitions of ancient and modern art from all over the world.

Many antiquities collections in Arab countries are registered with the government, and new policies for ownership are being considered. The sale and export of antiquities is controlled. However, no restrictions are imposed on private collections of more contemporary ethnographic or fine art objects, such as the internationally acclaimed Kawar collection of costume and weavings from the Arab world, owned by Widad Kawar of Jordan.

Museums, whether for art, archeology, or folklore, have been slow to develop in the Middle East for many reasons, leading Wijdan Ali, president of the Royal Society of Fine Arts in Jordan, to lament: "Art is not taken seriously, by either officials or the general public" (1990, 184). Publications about museums are few, although Ali has written articles in Arabic and English, and Rafik Lahham has written a series of historical articles in Arabic. Perhaps the most immediate reasons for this slow development have been economics and lack of interest, followed by demographic and population upheaval and political uncertainty because of the Israeli and Gulf wars. However, there are other more basic forces, both historical and contemporary, that have contributed to this slow development. Historically, there has been a general lack of interest by the people and the power structure in the monuments and relics that are so prevalent in the region.

The rise of Christianity dampened the desire to collect classical art, and throughout the Middle Ages objects from antiquity often were destroyed or disappeared for centuries. The Muslims generally had an attitude of benign neglect for the architectural monuments of previous cultures found in their territories and only began to appreciate and seriously preserve them some fifty years ago. This interest in the monuments of their heritage also coincides with the surge of interest in museums and private collecting.

Salah Stétié has offered several explanations for the relative disinterest existing in the Middle East in establishing museums and preserving historic sites. First of all, he argues, there is the psychological factor of "too much is too much: the Islamic peoples have had and still do have just too many admirable monuments." Second is "the spiritual factor of their rootlessness and the concept 'that all must return to dust.' " He also posits a cultural factor: that the underdevelopment resulting from successive invasions, occupations, and colonizations may have caused in the present inhabitants an "aesthetic sense [that has been] blunted or diminished," and a socioeconomic factor, which is underscored by continued illicit traffic in artifacts. Finally, he argues, there is the factor of societal change, in this case the transformation of spiritual values into the aesthetic ones of today's fast-moving, high-tech global society (Stétié 1982, 15–16).

Compounding all these factors is the misplaced perception of many popular writers that Arabs place very little value on presenting their past. In his book *The Haj*, for example, Leon Uris writes: "There is a Department of Antiquities in Jordan. The Department exists only to interest foreigners in coming to Jordan to dig. They take almost everything out" (1984, 37). This claim is, among other things, simplistic, and does not represent government policy. The government controls the movement of all antiquities.

If today's museums are a Western concept, how can they serve the needs and goals of non-Western societies? Are these Western-conceived institutions inappropriate because they reinforce a colonial mentality? Should museums be a vehicle to expose, condemn, and vanquish colonialist hegemony? Silas Okita argues: "Museums must help strengthen ethnic and national identities, but also should nourish collective humanity and equip the world's peoples to meet the contemporary challenges of human existence" (1997, 129–39).

This outlines a universal purpose for museums, but what about the more specific purpose of serving nationalistic needs? Museums now face many changes and challenges, especially in Jordan, where the new leadership will prompt shifts in Jordan's relations with its neighbors, Israel and the Palestinians. Museums can serve an important role, as Archabal points out, not only because they can house the past but also because they can capture the present for posterity (1998, 33). She recognizes that in times of change museums are important because they possess the accumulated experience of humankind; she gives credence to museums as keepers of the past because, as such, they not only give meaning and orientation to the current moment but also provide the energy to move into the future.

Museums in Jordan

> In every museum they need a woman. Man isn't able to do the arranging. Women, for care, are more capable.
>
> —*Zahida Safer*

Jordan's museums vary not only in size, condition, and quality but in their collections, amenities, and entrance fees. They also differ in governance and purpose. From the earliest, founded in Jerash in 1923, to the latest, Amman's Numismatic Museum of the Jordan National Bank, which opened in 2002, they seek different audiences, provide different programs, and have widely disparate budgets.

To be included in this study, a museum had to be nonprofit; it had to be designated as a museum by the government (specifically the Ministry of Culture or the Ministry of Tourism and Antiquities); and it had to be either sanctioned as a museum by the Department of Antiquities or currently operating through their programs and literature as a museum. In addition it had to be a formal institution with the primary intent of educating rather than just providing exhibition space, a sales gallery, or a warehouse of objects; it had to employ a professional staff; and it had to be open to the public on a regularly scheduled basis.

In this study, however, as in most seeking to apply a set of criteria, one exception was made: even though it exists only in print format and on the Internet, I included the Museum With No Frontiers since it is properly sanctioned, educational in purpose, and available on demand to those with the proper equipment. This cyber museum was created in 1995 during a meeting of the European Commission held to establish cultural relations among twelve Mediterranean countries. Each country was asked to adopt a specific historical period and represent it in the cyber museum. Jordan chose the Umayyad period.

These criteria did disqualify several institutions and sites, including the Petra Forum Museum in Wadi Musa at the Petra Forum Hotel complex. Although it contains artifacts in a sophisticated museum environment, it is not open to the public except upon request. Fortunately, the small one-room museum has a glass front allowing some objects to be viewed from outside. The Ministry of Tourism and Antiquities founded it in cooperation with the University of Florence and Brown University in order to present material from excavations of settlements relating to the Crusaders in the Holy Land.

Four more "museums" at the University of Jordan—the Animal, Botanical, Insect, and Medical Museums—were likewise omitted. Since their primary purpose is to serve students, they are properly "collections" rather then museums. Nabil Khairy, the university's vice dean, considers them "teaching collections," although the Botanical Museum is sometimes open to the public. A natural history museum moved to the University of Science and Technology from Yarmouk University in 1986, contains another study collection. Another university-sponsored museum not on the list is the one at Al al-Bayt University in Mafraq. Although it had representative archeological and ethnographic materials on loan, its presentations resembled a trade fair when I visited in 1996 as a participant in the Fifth International Seminar on Islamic Art and Architecture. The university was planning to establish a museum in the future. There is also a collection of archeological material in Azraq that does not qualify as a museum for this research.

Museums, like other institutions, achieve their goals using many methods and through many disciplines. In the United States one national organization, the American Association of Museums (AAM), is the umbrella spokesman for all museum disciplines. The listing in *The Official Museum Directory* of categories under its concern ranges from art museums and galleries to woodcarving museums. Likewise, Jordan's museums can be categorized in seven different disciplines: archeology, ethnography, fine arts, history, numismatics, philately, and science. The largest category is archeology, with sixteen museums, representing the desire of the Department of Antiquities to establish a museum at every major antiquities site. If this policy is continued, there will be more museums created in the future. As the second most prevalent category, ethnographic museums (sometimes called anthropological or heritage museums) present the artifacts of daily life such as costume, jewelry, weapons, tools, and utensils, and are the most likely to contain objects made by and for women. The third-largest category of museums is history. These museums, often in historic buildings, present regional history since the Hejira, usually focusing on the lives of early Hashemite notables, their memorabilia, and their contribution to the modern state of Jordan.

The remaining museums—most often private—collect and present objects in the disciplines of the physical sciences and fine arts as well as objects such as coins, stamps, and religious items. The exceptions are the Geological Museum and the Postal Museum, which are maintained by government ministries, and the aquarium, which is administered by the University of Jordan.

What do Jordan's museums and art centers look like? Do they resemble the imitation Greek temples found in Europe and the United States? Many are incorporated into existing ancient sites: the Folklore Museum and the Museum of Popular Traditions are located at the sides of the Roman theater in downtown Amman, for example, and the Petra Archeological Museum was built in the al-Habis Mountain at Petra. Others have been installed in creatively adapted older buildings—houses, railroad stations, and castles. An old Turkish fort in Irbid, for example, is being renovated to house a new archeological museum, while a villa in Salt has been modified to house the Museum of Folklore and the Museum of Archeology. The offices and galleries of the Darat al Funun complex are sited in renovated homes, while the floor of an ancient Roman temple forms its performing arts stage. The former home of an art patron has been renovated to house the Jordan National Gallery, and at the University of Jordan, the first classroom building on campus has been modified to house the Archeological Museum. Al al-Bayt University in Mafraq is likewise planning to house a new museum in a former air force building, and the towns of Mafraq, Aqaba, and Umm Qais have converted Ottoman-era homes to galleries and museums.

Often, the adaptation of old buildings for new purposes yields double benefit, saving buildings of cultural and architectural merit while providing a home for museum or gallery collections. In some cases, however, it is not the wisest choice. As curator Eman Oweis from Jerash expressed it, "We have often been compelled to use old buildings designed in the nineteenth and early twentieth centuries as museums; they are thus inappropriate for the purpose because they have not been designed to preserve archeological objects" (1994, 171). Her comments on the inadequacy of such arrangements are echoed in a broader discussion by Pieterse, who targets inappropriate readaptive use of buildings "which turn life-worlds into spectacle, for instance by reconverting the use of buildings—turning mosques into discos or restaurants" (1995, 68).

As I attempted to organize and simplify data by grouping, difficulties arose in categorizing some of the museums into discipline-based areas: archeology, ethnography, science, art, religion, and history. The Islamic Museum in the King Abdullah Mosque, for example, contains ancient objects, yet also focuses on the personal effects of King Abdullah I. In spite of its name and location, I decided to put this museum in the historical category. Likewise, while the Museum of Jordanian Heritage (in the Institute of Archeology and Anthropology at Yarmouk University) contains presentations of early Islamic and nineteenth-century ethnographic objects, it also contains dioramas of a potter's shop, blacksmith's workshop, and pharmacy, as well as many archeological exhibits. The introduction to the museum catalog explains this mixture by declaring that "the museum aims to present the historical development of the region, with a focus on the relations and correlations of natural, demographic, socioeconomic and cultural facts. Therefore, no major break occurs in the transition from the archeological to the ethnographical exhibits" (13). It was included in the ethnographic museum category.

An analysis of the disciplines of Jordan's thirty-six museums reveals that sixteen of them are archeological; following this, six are ethnographic, five historical, two contemporary art, three science, one religious, one numismatic, one virtual, and one philatelic. Eighteen are governed by the Department of Antiquities, six are affiliated with a university, five are private, five are administered by various agencies of the government, and two are under the governance of the Department of al-Waqf that administers and protects Islamic buildings and holy places.

Future Museums

In contrast to the structured routine of existing museums, some museums in development at the time of writing exude swirls of controversy, frustration, or excitement: the on-again, off-again cliffhangers in the development of the National Museum, its reality morphed through more than two decades of rhetoric, dreams, and strained friendships; the heavy, plodding momentum of the Hijaz Railway Museum, which touts not only history but entertainment rail tie by rail tie; the fleeting reality, feasibility, and economics involved in vying for collections for a museum in Abu Obeida; the readaptive project destined to make an educational center out of the old parliament building; the fortuitous meeting of the minds between big business and philanthropy wherein dream became reality for the Jordan National Bank's Numismatic Museum; and the proud heritage locked in a small room awaiting action at the Circassian Center for Cultural Heritage. These six projects do not exhaust the list; two others are also on the drawing board. Tradition and respect for order and public security will found and fund the new police museum, and the challenge to bring life to the Dead Sea will inspire the development of an educational museum that represents this environmentally sensitive area.

These eight museums represent the initiatives of many people and committees, and a great deal of time, thought, and money. Discussion of their problems and passions gives an idea of the difficulties in establishing museums in a developing country—and at the same time reveals the universality of people's needs and dreams.

In addition to these new museums, three others have been proposed, two of them the brainchildren of women. The first, a proposal for a children's musem, is a project of Queen Rania, who has an active interest in museums and the arts. Plans for its construction at the new Al Hussein Park in Amman called for completion sometime in 2003. The second proposal, for a museum for the disabled, was announced in an article by Nesreen Al-Tal through the International Council of Museums (ICOM) (1994, 141–42). The proposal does not specify a location or date for completion, but it does describe the need for an institution devoted to the physically challenged. It also outlines its goals, purpose, physical infrastructure, and displays. Lastly, a museum is being proposed that would exhibit the archeology of the area around Mt. Nebo.

Will these new and proposed museums be different from those already in service? How will they differ? A new facility obviously offers new opportunities for physical accommodation of people, for innovation, and new technologies. To the envy of the staff of preexisting museums, these new museums will be able to go directly to the present, bypassing the problems of the old, especially if they can attract funding from outside patrons or nongovernmental sources.

Further expansion of the number, diversity, and variety of museums may come if the government decides to allow private collectors to open their own museums. The issue is under discussion at the Department of Antiquities. The majority of women curators, administrators, collectors, and arts activists in this study responded positively to the issue.

How has Jordan, with its limited resources, been able to support new museums? How can a country with needs so diverse, so basic, aspire realistically to the establishment of museums? One of the ways Jordan is able to develop its cultural resources is through support, generous donations, and loans from other governments, nongovernmental organizations (NGOs), and international institutions. Many countries maintain cultural centers in Amman that help support the local arts, including the American Center, Goethe Institute, French Cultural Center, British Council, Turkish Cultural Center, and Spanish Cultural Center. International organizations, such as the AAM, ICOM, United Nations Educational, Scientific, and Cultural Organization (UNESCO), the Arab League Educational, Cultural, and Scientific Organization (ALECSO), Islamic Educational, Scientific, and Cultural Organization (ISESCO), and ICOM-ARAB, set standards, supply information and expertise, and fund cultural initiatives. Other organizations, such as the Japan International Cooperation Agency (JICA) and the United States Information Service (USIS), have provided funding for specific museum projects, from buildings to educational services.

Although the government may have desired and planned museums throughout the country, it was often private enterprise and foreign support and expertise that initiated them and made them a reality. The British have long played an important role in the development of cultural activities. Affiliations with British museums, archeological institutes, and cultural councils guided the early establishment of museums, such as the Jerash Archeological Museum and the Jordan Archeological Museum in Amman.

Driving all of these plans, dreams, and activities have been the people: the colorful, impassioned, dedicated, altruistic, glory-hungry, eccentric, visionary people of Jordan. Many of them have been women. Records from the past reveal the same names over and over, names of people who worked tirelessly—as committee members, workers, helpers, supporters, and advisers—to establish Jordan's public and private museums. They include women like Wijdan Ali, founder of the Jordan National Gallery, formerly affiliated with the museum at the Central Bank, a consultant and donor to the university's National Heritage Museum, and a university dean; Suha Shoman, founder of the Darat al Funun, who, among many other activities, served on the National Gallery board; and Widad Kawar, Hind Nasser, and Samia Zaru, advisers and board members for several museums. Artist and art educator Samia Zaru recalled early meetings in the 1970s with Wijdan Ali; the two would meet in their homes, sometimes with children in their arms, and make plans for the Jordan National Gallery. Collector and author Widad Kawar has participated on many citizen advisory boards over the years. Her extensive collection of embroidered costumes and weavings has been on loan to several international museums and is well published.

There were men, too; even though this research focuses on women, several of these men merit mention. Hind Nasser (1999) recalls working with several men on museum committees: Ghazi Bisheh, former director general of antiquities; Moawiyah Ibrahim from Yarmouk University; Hisham Khalib, lecturer and collector; Taleb Rifa'i and Jafar Tukan, architects; Khier Yassin; and archeologist Fawzi Zayeddin.

I have identified thirty-six museums currently operating in Jordan, eight that are being developed, and three that are being proposed. But ideas did not stop with these entities. Everywhere I inquired, there were dreams—ideas—for new museums. For instance, Ministry of Communication personnel spoke of developing a museum of communication that would feature old telephones and telecom devices.

The following Jordanian museums are under development at the time of this writing:

The Abu Obeida (Ubida) Museum, Jordan Valley

The Ministry of Awqaf, Islamic Affairs, and Holy Places is proposing a new museum for this Jordan Valley site. The ministry has requested Islamic-period objects from the Department of Antiquities for the collection and proposes using an existing building that contains a small hall with wall niches where items could be displayed. The project is under consideration. If the department's collections are not available, the future is uncertain unless donations can be secured or the appropriate objects purchased.

The Circassian Museum
(the Circassian Center for Cultural Heritage), Amman

The Circassian community in Amman has been collecting objects of folklore and heritage for several years in hopes of preserving them and eventually establishing a museum. Presently the collection, of perhaps eighty-five pieces, is stored at the office complex of the Circassian Welfare Society, an organization that was originally established in 1932. Administrator for the project is Muhammed Ali Werdan.

Although there is no active campaign drive for the project at the moment, the collection contains utilitarian objects, farm equipment and tools, household implements, baskets, drinking horns, samovars, costumes, photographs, and weavings.

The Dead Sea Museum

The Dead Sea area is believed to be the site of five biblical cities: Sodom, Gomorrah, Admah, Zebouin, and Zoar. The eastern shore has changed little since ancient times, and a call for a museum of the desert was made in 1994 during the ICOM conference in Amman. Because the desert is a common element in most Arab countries, the exhibits could be developed in a mobile format and be shared. The new museum will showcase the geology, flora and fauna, history, and natural products of the Dead Sea. The focus of the museum will be on the unique environment of the region, its long history of human habitation, and its potential in the twenty-first century. The project is being coordinated with the Ministry of Tourism and Antiquities with the support of JICA.

Secretary-General Alia Hatough Bouran of the Ministry of Tourism and Antiquities, who is interested in environmental issues in Jordan, envisions it as a living museum. Asked about the museum's programs, and how women would participate or be represented in it, she responded: "We don't want to relate women just to the house. . . . They will be represented in teaching, industry, pharmaceuticals, and various industries" (Bouran 1999).

Hijaz (Hedjazi) Railway Museum, Amman

For Muslims, the tenets of Islam include a pilgrimage to the holy city of Mecca at least once in their lifetime, if possible. In the past, this travel has been difficult and often hazardous. The Ottomans built the Hijaz Railway, with six stations, through Jordan to facilitate *haj* travel to Medina. This line through Jordan shortened the trip between Damascus and Medina from forty days to three days. Completed in 1908, the rail system also linked Amman with Syria and Palestine. Interestingly, in 1999, the government issued stamps depicting the Hijaz Railway. The stamps show a map of Jordan with ten stations along the route.

To reach the future railway museum, located at the old train station, one goes through the industrial section of downtown Amman, an area called Mahatta. The current office, yard, maintenance areas, and storage buildings are secured on a site bounded by hills and two main roads. Once inside the enclave, the rest of the city vanishes and one is transported visually into another time period. Three antique twentieth-century train engines rest on sidetracks; a newer diesel purrs nearby. Small flower gardens dot areas between the tracks and working areas.

Diesel trains run today from the station, and short tourist excursions can be arranged going both north and south out of the capital. But the tourist and educational potential of the station and museum has not been developed. On the day of my arrival, a group of schoolchildren had just left in a train to Mafraq for a picnic. Railroad memorabilia and ephemera are presently on display in the office building across the train yard from the proposed museum. A wall-mounted train model and a case of small objects including lamps, brass uniform buttons, a telephone, tickets, timetables, stamps, inkwells, and insignias are displayed in the foyer. Old photographs of the station and the Ottoman trains line the corridor walls, and in a humorous personal touch, wooden signs in the shape of trains hang beside open doors of the offices to identify the occupants. In a most appealingly focused office, the director conducts business amid train archives, books, and art. Visitors are treated to a circular track and model train as they sit around his coffee table.

A red tile roof distinguishes the proposed museum from the office building. It is actually the former station house, but for years it has been used for storage. Inside the one-room building, the plated metal cage for passenger separation and the original wall safe remain. The original basalt rock flooring has been exposed, and a loft area at one end will add additional exhibit space to the small facility.

The National Museum, Amman

The National Museum should be autonomous, or semi-autonomous. Like the
universities, with its own board, with a steering committee and executive
committee.

—*Alia Hatough Bouran*

In 1996, JICA published *The Study on the Tourism Development Plan in the
Hashemite Kingdom of Jordan.* In its final report, economic and educational
goals and benefits were stressed, including tourism and urban revitalization. The final report reflects the findings of July 1995 when a private committee prepared a preliminary concept for the new museum, with a
twelve-thousand-square-meter building and timeline, budget, and training
needs. The study also referenced a national museums institute that would
be created to train staff. A rendering of the new facility features a large
square building with a recessed front entrance and a pyramid on top. The
total cost estimate for the project was put at $14.5 million.

The *Jordan National Museum Conceptual Plan* was published in 1997
(Sims and Rogan 1997). This major museum would be a state-of-the-art
jewel crowning the monarchy and representing the history and culture of
Jordan. Hind Nasser was chair of the committee. The plan proposed a
three-year development schedule with a scheduled opening in February
2000. That goal was not met. James Sims and Patrick Rogan proposed three
development phases and included a staff of thirty-nine to run the facility.
Total cost for the project was $20,456,200. Visual rendering of this plan
showed several square wings attached to a larger central building that was
crowned with a large shallow dome (Sims and Rogan 1997).

After many years of discussion and planning, dreams were on their way
to achievement. In January 1999, the *Star,* a Jordanian weekly newspaper,
reported the signing of a new tourism agreement between Japan and Jordan
while Prime Minister Masahiko Koumura was visiting the country. The
Star announced that "Jordan recently received aid from Japan to develop a
number of tourist sites in different areas in the Kingdom. The cost of these
tourist projects will involve the development of the capital through the establishment of a National Museum in the Ras Al Ain area. Another project
will involve the city of Salt, where a popular museum and a visitors' center
will be established. A touristic road between the Dead Sea and the Ma'in

Spa will also be constructed, in addition to a nature museum for the Dead Sea area."

JICA is no stranger to support of cultural activities in Jordan. The agency had previously donated equipment, through the Noor Al Hussein Foundation, to the planetarium at the Haya Cultural Center. Japanese economic aid to Jordan began in 1974 through the Official Development Assistance (ODA) Programme, and the country has been one of Jordan's largest foreign donors.

The need for a national museum, a showcase of Jordanian history and culture, has been recognized for more than twenty years. The former director general of antiquities, Ghazi Bisheh (1999), recalled that he had been involved in the planning since 1978. The first site proposal for the project was prepared by Crystal Bennet, from the British Museum. There have been several other studies in the past, one tying the new museum together with the existing Archeological Museum at the Citadel, in a triangular complex that included the Nympheum and the Roman Theater in downtown Amman via an overhead funicular.

Over the years, several sites were discussed and several committees formed. Architect Jafar Tukan (1998) recalled working on small committees for the design of the museum while on the city council, when a municipal park site was proposed near the palace area and introduced into the master plan. James Sims was hired by the Ministry of Tourism to propose an interactive museum, but the plans stalled because of lack of funding.

Another site proposed for the museum was in the fast-growing area between Sports City and the University of Jordan. In an undated *Working Paper on the National Museum*, the Ministry of Tourism and Antiquities outlined the goals for the national museum, argued the rationale for an enlarged archeology museum, and provided some suggestion for its development. The paper contained a critique of the inadequacies of the Archeological Museum at the Citadel, and argued that the new museum be "on the outskirts of Amman . . . between Sports City and the University of Jordan" (n.d., 4). It also proposed basic facilities for the public, research, and storage areas without giving details of size and cost. Like many others, Nabil Khairy of the Department of Archeology at the University of Jordan agreed with this suggestion: "Downtown—it's crowded, dirty—no parking . . . there are no shops there" (1999).

The present site in Ras al Ain is in the recently built municipal center complex that contains a mosque, garden, and city hall. It is within walking distance of the Roman Theater and the Nympheum. With JICA support, the museum was slated to begin groundbreaking in September 1999 (Bermamet 1999).

ROM Cultural Innovations proposed a concept entitled "Amman 2010: City of Today with Roots in History," wherein the new museum becomes a cornerstone of the revitalization for the area of City Hall and would eventually incorporate an IMAX theater and restaurants.

The decision to locate the museum in the Ras al Ain area of downtown makes the proposed museum important to an overall urban core renewal plan that will invigorate community-based commercial and cultural development in the area and attract and hold visitors. The project would "retain the special character of the cityscape while integrating and focusing visitor activities in a pedestrian zone of multi-use facilities, entertainment, education and services" (ROM Cultural Innovations n.d.).

The new national museum means different things to different people. To some, it is the culmination of a long, well-fought battle to secure funding for a showcase of Jordanian culture. To others, it is the symbol of Jordan's arrival into the twenty-first century. To many, it is a way of enhancing Jordan's undeveloped tourism industry. But even as groundbreaking begins, issues beyond funding and site have vexed the planning committees, issues such as governance, collections, and staffing. Should the museum be governed by the Ministry of Tourism and Antiquities, by the Department of Antiquities, by a specially appointed association that includes representatives of the ministries, or a board appointed by the prime minister and representatives of the municipality of Amman? As for the staff, should they be employees of the Department of Antiquities or experts affiliated with the University of Jordan? Should they be specially trained in museology and administration without an archeological background?

And what should the museum collect? When John Cotton Dana posed that question, his own answer was: "First of all, ideas" (1917, 35). Current plans for the national museum aim for it to be diverse, including objects representative of antiquity to contemporary times; to include archeology, geology, and historical exhibits, and perhaps even the fine arts. There is even discussion of incorporating the collections of the Jordan Archeological Museum, freeing that museum complex for other governmental services, perhaps a visitor center.

During an interview, Nidal Al-Hadid, the mayor of Amman, discussed his involvement with the development of the museum and identified members of the team currently working on the committee, including Rima Kha-laf Hunaidi, the minister of planning; Aqel Beltaji, the minister of tourism and antiquities; and Shadah Abu Hadeb, the municipal planning represen-tative. From the balcony of his second-floor office, the mayor pointed to the site on the municipal island between a fountain and a mosque. His office was a beehive of constant activity, with staff consulting and interrupting and guests arriving for coffee and being seated on the couches in the screen-divided room. A huge color photograph of Amman at night dazzled the visitor, and the *Encyclopedia Britannica* resided in the bookcase behind his desk. Several phones continuously rang, beeped, and sang. Energetic, mul-titasking while answering my questions about the museum, he was specific about its audience: "It's for tourists, and the things they want . . . the prod-ucts, handicrafts, glass, Bani Hameda. Our audience will be tourists. Our people see this every day. So our main audience will be tourists" (Al-Hadid 1998).

Numismatic Museum of the Jordan National Bank, Amman

Founded in 1999 by the Jordan National Bank, the museum houses the collection of Nayef Goussous, who remains the curator. The museum was scheduled to open in 2001, however, a new site delayed its opening until 2002. The mission of the museum is to educate people about their heritage, to teach about the interrelationships of peoples, and to conserve coins. The international collection consists of over nine thousand coins, medals, beads, paper money, weights, and carved gems. The exhibit area is designed to be state of the art. In addition to the exhibit area, which can be reconfigured by moveable cases, there is a separate reference library and research room. Collectors, students, and scholars are encouraged to use the library. Publi-cations about the collections are planned. Another dimension to the educa-tional programming being planned is a lecture series that will take place in an audiovisual conference room. There is presently a full-time staff of two.

The Police Museum (Museum of Public Security), Amman

Members of the public security forces in Amman are planning a museum that will tell the history of their service to the country. The three-thousand-square-meter building being proposed is at the police academy in Amman, a site that would preclude public visitation because access would be restricted and by permission only.

The displays would focus on the history of the public security forces; the collections would include mannequins in uniform, medals, citations, and weapons as well as documentation relating to specific people and events in the domain of security, such as who was the first policeman in the kingdom and what was the first recorded crime. Photographs and security memorabilia would be a large part of the displays.

Museum of Political History (Museum of the Political History of HM the Late King Abdullah I bin Al Hussein), Amman

The old parliament building between the First and Second Circles in Amman is being transformed by the Ministry of Culture into a museum devoted to the achievements of King Abdullah I. The facility contains offices, a lecture hall, and a museum with King Abdullah's books, memorabilia, photographs, documents, and examples of his poetry from the period 1921 to 1951.

The Ministry of Culture claims its mission is to maintain and record the specific historical period established and supported by King Abdullah bin Al Hussein; to introduce generations to the history of the founder of the kingdom and the role he played in various fields of science and knowledge, and to acquaint people with the leading personalities of the kingdom who had a role in supporting the founder. Originally scheduled to open in 2000, it was not yet open at the time of writing.

Affiliated and Support Institutions

Mention should be made of the affiliated institutions that support and interact with museums in Amman. Early cultural clubs, such as the Scientific Nahda Institute and Cultural Cooperation Club in Amman and the U'ruba School in Irbid, presented exhibitions and other cultural programming. Institutions created later include the Princess Fakhr Al Nisa Zeid Gallery at the Ministry of Culture, the Jordan Plastic Art Association, the Archeological Gallery at the Department of Antiquities, and the Royal Cultural Center. These and other nonprofit organizations, such as the Abdel Hameed Shoman Foundation, support the visual arts through events and publications and provide information resources on museum-related issues. Cultural and research centers operated by foreign consulates, missions, embassies, and scientific organizations also support the visual arts through exhibitions, reference libraries, and training opportunities.

The Jordan Plastic Art Association (Gallery of the Plastic Artists Union). The Jordan Plastic Art Association, currently under the direction of Khalid Khrais, was established in 1978, moving in 1995 to an old house on Jebel Weibde that has been converted to a gallery. The association held its first exhibition in 1979. Before this, in the 1970s, the Ministry of Culture supported the establishment of the Center of Fine Arts, where artists such as Mohanna Durra, Ali al Goul, Rafik Lahham, Kuram al-Nimri, and others held art classes, programs, and meetings.

The association's purpose is to exhibit the works of Jordanian artists in the country and abroad. Many consider the association to have been the incubator of Jordan's early art scene. There are approximately three hundred and fifty members of the association; membership is ten Jordanian dinars (JD) annually, and a board determines the exhibit schedule and membership roster. The gallery has only three small rooms, but an adjoining outside patio allows more public and artistic interaction.

The Exhibition Gallery of Arab Heritage and Recent Discoveries. Inaugurated by Queen Noor in 1992, the exhibition gallery inside the Department of Antiquities headquarters on Jebel Amman focused on displaying recent archeological discoveries from excavations in Jordan. This temporary gallery served as a research and publication center for works before they were placed in more appropriate museums throughout the country. Displays have included Byzantine and early Islamic mosaics, replicas of architecture from Petra, and a collection of Safaitic and Kufic inscriptions. The gallery operates sporadically; the displays exist according to the needs of the department.

Princess Fakhr Al Nisa Zeid Gallery. The Ministry of Culture maintains many facilities throughout the country, including art centers and libraries. In Amman, along with the Fine Arts Training Center, the ministry supports the visual arts through the Princess Fakhr Al Nisa Zeid Gallery in its building on Wasfi al Tal Street. Named after Turkish artist and art teacher Fahrelnissa Zeid (related to the Jordanian monarchy), the gallery is located on the ground floor and is accessed from a side street. The gallery opened in 1997 with an exhibition of Fahrelnissa's works and now contains selections from the ministry's collection of paintings, graphics, ceramics, and sculpture. Many of the works date from the 1970s, giving the collection historical importance. The permanent exhibition has no checklist, and there are few labels on the walls.

The aims of the gallery are:

- to document the history of the Jordan plastic art movement;
- to create an information center for plastic arts;
- to give the opportunity to the Jordanian public to see a selection of artistic creation;
- to hold cultural and art criticism lectures (exhibits, videotapes, and slides);
- to hold Jordanian and Arab art exhibitions; and
- to strengthen the relationship between art works and the public (Al Ameri n.d.).

A color brochure documents the opening of the gallery, describing the life and works of Fahrelnissa Zeid and the aims of the gallery and summarizing the plastic art movement in Jordan.

The Royal Cultural Center. The Royal Cultural Center in Amman opened in 1982 as a showcase of the visual and performing arts. It contains the Royal Theater, the Studio Theater, a conference hall, and several side hallways and rooms that are used for exhibition purposes. Activities in the center include painting and sculpture exhibitions, musical performances, theater, film presentations, conferences, and lectures (Bisharat 1984).

Support of the visual arts comes from many sources. Already mentioned are the programs sponsored by local and regional businesses, nonprofits, and foreign cultural centers. Jordanian businesses, both private and government affiliated, began to play a serious role in the support of the fine arts in the 1980s. Mirroring the early museum development in Turkey, the business community assumed leadership in support for the arts.

Other Visual Arts Opportunities

Royal Jordanian Airlines opened the Alia Gallery in 1980; several banks helped to develop visual arts awareness, including the Petra Bank, which began collecting and presenting art in its 1983 gallery at the bank's headquarters. The Central Bank of Jordan also developed a small collection, and the Arab Bank, under the Abdel Hameed Shoman Foundation, opened a gallery in 1988.

Several galleries of contemporary art have opened in Amman, but their success and longevity have been limited. In its inaugural catalog, the Gallery at the Ministry of Culture referred to more than eighteen galleries that existed in Amman in the 1980s. In 1981, *UR* magazine credited Amman with "some twenty exhibitions" (Mostyn 1981/2, 79), while in 1994, according to Ayed, "there were five hundred and fifty art exhibits held in Jordan" (1996, 82).

The earliest gallery to open in Amman was The Gallery at the Jordan Intercontinental Hotel. Directed by Nuha Batchone since 1972, it still operates with a selection of contemporary local and regional artists in its stable. Other galleries of fine art in Amman in 1999 include: Ab'ad Art Gallery, Al Anda Gallery, Arts Centre, Baladna Art Gallery, Hammourabi Art Gallery, Haya Arts Center, Jordan Design and Trade Center, Al Mashreq Gallery, Nabataeans Gallery, Orfali Art Gallery, Orient Gallery, and the Phoenix Gallery. Additional venue space for the visual arts can be found in hotels and bookstores, at design centers such as Artisana and the Jordan Design and Trade Center, at City Hall and occasionally at the Underpass Gallery, the pedestrian underpass opposite the entrance to the University of Jordan that operates when the Amman municipality can supply a guard.

Abbreviations

AAM	American Association of Museums
ALECSO	Arab League Educational, Cultural, and Scientific Organization
ASG	Ahliyyah School for Girls
ICOM	International Council of Museums
IPAM	International Partners among Museums
ISESCO	Islamic Educational, Scientific, and Cultural Organization
JICA	Japan International Cooperation Agency
JNCW	Jordanian National Commission for Women
JNFW	Jordanian National Forum for Women
JWU	Jordanian Women's Union
MENA	Middle East and North Africa
NGO	nongovernmental organization
UNESCO	United Nations Educational, Scientific, and Cultural Organization
UNRWA	United Nations Relief Works Agency

WOMEN'S VOICES IN
MIDDLE EAST MUSEUMS

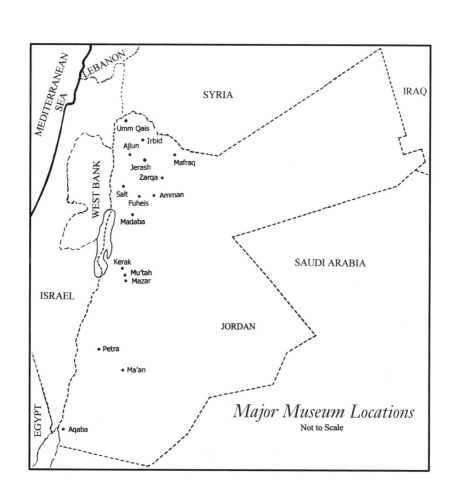

MEDITERRANEAN SEA

LEBANON

SYRIA

IRAQ

WEST BANK

• Umm Qais
• Irbid
Ajlun
• Mafraq
Jerash
Zarqa •
Salt •
• Amman
Fuheis
• Madaba

Kerak •
• Mu'tah
• Mazar

ISRAEL

SAUDI ARABIA

JORDAN

• Petra

• Ma'an

EGYPT

• Aqaba

Major Museum Locations
Not to Scale

1

Women in Middle Eastern Society

Cultural Overview

If real change is to occur in a society, it has to start from the grass roots.
—Basma bint Talal

A majority of Jordan's 5.5 million people are Arab and Muslim, and trace their roots to Palestine. Of the remainder, some are descended from Bedouin Arabs and others from the various minorities from the Caucasus. About 80 percent of the total population lives in urban areas. Nomadic and seminomadic Bedouins inhabit the desert areas. Roughly 5 percent of Jordanians are Christians, most of whom live in Madaba, Kerak, Salt, Ajlun, and Amman. Jordan also hosts a considerable population of Palestinian refugees—nearly 1.6 million in 2000, according to the United Nations Relief Works Agency (UNRWA). Of these, about 20 percent live in camps administered by the UNRWA, while the rest are scattered throughout the kingdom, with large groups living in the cities of Amman and Irbid.

Anthropologists have often likened the mix of peoples in Jordan to a mosaic, in which each ethnic group retains its distinct identity yet contributes to the overall picture of the society. However, given the changes brought by increasing social and economic integration, Jordan's societal design might be more usefully described as moiré, where patterns are obvious but can shift or blend in interaction.

In the Middle East the role of women as workers outside the home has continuously shifted over the centuries, expanding or diminishing as the economics and customs of the area changed. The degree of participation by

3

women in the work force has also varied according to social status and ethnic or tribal affiliation.

Historians describe three types of restrictions that affect women's lives in Muslim societies. The first category consists of restrictions found in the Qur'an, Hadith, Sunna, and *Shari'a* law codes; these affect inheritance, marriage, divorce, children, and witnessing. The second category consists of those restrictions imposed by the practice of seclusion, which limits public access for women. The third category consists of behavioral controls arising from societal norms and traditions. Since these restrictions rely on social pressure, they are more subtle than the first two types, but often prove the most constricting.

Historically, women came to be excluded from the power structure as society became economically divided into public and private sectors. Eventually traditions and customs became entrenched, solidifying the separateness of these domains.

Nashat suggests that during the first century of Islam, Muslim women were active in the workforce, but gradually found their roles constricted as time passed (1995, 4). Although patterns of seclusion and repression predate Islam in the region, social and economic changes—particularly the rise of urbanism—dramatically altered the treatment of women and limited their access to opportunities. Such restrictions on women's roles gradually gained legitimacy and were encouraged in response to discrepancies in Islamic law.

The subordination of women in Islamic societies, then, appears to have resulted from the gradual evolution of social and economic conditions from Neolithic times. When agriculture was the major source of family livelihood, women participated in the labor force while also having responsibility for domestic life. Urbanism changed this balance. By undermining their economic power, it relegated women to an inferior position—and eventually to one favoring seclusion.

However, women choosing to participate in the workforce today can find justification for their cause in early Islam. The prophet Muhammad was employed by and later married Khadijah bint Khuwaylid, a twice-widowed woman whose Arabian caravans traded with Syria. After her death, Muhammad married again. His last wife, Aisha, played a major role in politics in Mecca, even accompanying an army into battle. Other women in the first centuries of Islam who were part of the work force and achieved fame may likewise serve as examples to women today. Nevertheless, famous as many of them were, most are identified either as the mother of a male child or as the daughter of a man, not by their own given names.

In early Muslim history, occupations for women after the seventh century included bath attendant, matchmaker, trader to the harem, hairdresser, midwife, body washer, professional mourner, and weaver. Women were also active in the visual, written, and performing arts as poets, singers, dancers, clothing designers, and seamstresses. These occupations do not represent important jobs in the leadership of nations, however, and we know little about gender issues or women's equality from records of the ancient past.

Although women had achieved recognition for their work in specialized professions since pre-Islamic times, it was not until the nineteenth century that intellectuals and the emerging middle class began to advocate the public education of women. Publications such as the Turkish pamphlet "Kadinlar" (Women) by Semseddin Sami and the Egyptian book *Tahrir al-mar'a* (The emancipation of women) by Qasim Amin argued for this position. In the early twentieth century in the Middle East (and in the 1970s in Jordan), women's equality, education, and importance in the workforce came to the forefront. In concert with the establishment of museums and art centers in the Middle East, intellectual centers and their concern with gender issues first developed in Istanbul, Cairo, Damascus, and Beirut.

By the 1920s, the education of women, whether at home or in secondary schools, had become accepted in the liberal families of the middle and upper classes. Women were encouraged to become leaders, even administrators, in the segregated women's educational systems, and within these systems, higher education became available. The Western tradition of formal education was introduced in the Ottoman Empire in the nineteenth century. In 1866, Daniel Bliss established the American University of Beirut (formerly the Syrian Protestant College), and in 1900 the ancient Darulfunun (founded 1453) was reorganized to become the University of Istanbul, finally becoming Istanbul University in 1933. By World War I several colleges had been established, and in 1926 Damascus University allowed women into the faculties of medicine, law, and arts. That same year, the American University of Beirut, which had begun with sixteen students in a rented house, became coeducational, although until 1951, female students had to take their first two years at Beirut College for Women. The American University of Cairo admitted women in 1929, and the University of Jordan, established by royal decree in 1962 with the Faculty of Arts, had an initial coeducational enrollment of 167 students and eight faculty.

If the pace of change seems halting, it is largely because the subject of women's access to higher education, suffrage, and the opportunity to hold office has long been intertwined with religious, political, and family issues. Some conservative religious thinkers oppose such opportunities for women as contrary to the precedent set by the moral, social, and economic practices of the early Islamic communities. Fundamentalist groups have added legitimacy to this position by linking the role of women to issues of colonialism and imperialism, and to public resentment of Western values. Also interacting with and reinforcing this position are societal norms identifying women with the family and the concept of 'ird—the viewing of women as the repository of family honor.

According to Mernissi, historians interpret the somewhat cyclical resurgence of traditional rhetoric as a reflex of ruling groups threatened by acute and deep processes of change. "The problem Arab societies face is not whether to change, but how fast to change" (1987, 176). Jordan, like other Arab countries, is destined to change, no matter how loud its claim to uphold the "prestigious past" as the path to modernity.

The "woman question" is not a myth from *One Thousand and One Nights* with a happy ending. Several women in my study spoke of the patriarchal system that both constrains them and defines them as part of their tradition. Yuval-Davis defines the word *patriarchy* as the "autonomous system of women's subordination in society" (1997, 6). The concept of the dominant male and protective father exists in women's lives from the personal to the governmental level, from within their own homes to their country's monarchy, as in the public image of the late King Hussein as the father or patriarch of Jordan.

The system keeping women "in their place" in the Middle East, legitimized by the patriarchal religions of the region, whether Muslim, Hebrew, or Christian, has both advantages and disadvantages for those women. Many women maintain that it gives them the comfort of understanding their place in society: they know that their identity is clear and that their religion allows them spiritual inspiration. However, the system also justifies and perpetuates male control. Many women actually participate in this process, perpetuating male social control through the conformity of their behavior, role stereotyping, and dress, because it is comfortable, safe, and traditional.

Are women's status and opportunity governed by the socioeconomic system, or by religion? There are differing opinions. A great many women believe that everything—culture, politics, education, economics, and daily life—belongs to the realm of Islam. It is a way of life. Islam was responsible for unifying the divergent peoples of this area in the past, and it continues to forge a modern Jordanian society today. Tucker states that although much discussion of gender has taken on explicitly religious form, women themselves have tended to focus on constraints imposed by custom and tradition (1988, 93). From each perspective, it would be wrong to generalize about women or women's issues, for women and their situations are diverse, personal, and changing. Although patterns of participation or restriction can be recognized, not all women acknowledge the repression of the female in their society, nor is repression specific to the Middle East.

Among these opinions is that of Wijdan Ali. She contends that a Middle Eastern woman has no more difficulty in achieving her goals than a Western woman, and maintains that an educated woman in an Islamic society has ample opportunity to fulfill herself. "In many Islamic countries, from Lebanon, Iraq, and Egypt to Bangladesh and Pakistan, women became diplomats and prime ministers long before Margaret Thatcher in Britain. In our society the problem is not Islam versus women, but women versus themselves" (De Maio 1998, 2).

Barakat, in his broad discussion of religion, identity, and social class, concludes that while the Arab world is not shaped only by Islam, neither can it be interpreted through discussion of a "mosaic" society, for it operates in an arena of opposition: tribalism versus urbanism, unity versus fragmentation, the sacred versus the secular, familial loyalties versus national ones, and women versus men (1993).

2

Women in Jordan

Education

I felt no restraints as a woman. My family believed in education. My aunt, now ninety-three, used to be a teacher.

—*Suha Shoman*

In the late nineteenth and early twentieth centuries, religious groups and educational foundations established several private schools for girls in the West Bank. Foremost among them was the American Friends Girls School in Ramallah. It merged with the American Friends Boys School in Ramallah and today operates coeducationally. In 1944–45, Palestinian educator Abdul-Latif Tibawi, who worked in the Palestinian Education Department under the British Mandate, was concerned that there was little pressure for the education of girls. He noted that, of four hundred government village schools, only forty-six were for girls, with a total of 3,392 female pupils compared with 38,760 boys. The reason for this, he assumed, was the lack of training of women teachers. After 1948, both Jordan and UNRWA established schools in the area.

During the Ottoman era, there were no government schools in the area now forming Jordan; however, there were local schools called *kuttab*s and *madrasa*s, religious schools whose origins go back to early Islamic times. The first public school in Jordan's East Bank was built by the townspeople of Salt in 1923 and was limited to the education of boys. In 1926 in Amman, the Christian Mission Society of England established a private girls' school. Now called the Ahliyyah School for Girls, it serves 1,250 students in the kindergarten, elementary, and secondary divisions.

8

Today in Jordan there are three types of schools: those run by the government, those run by UNRWA, and those that are private. There are three divisions in the system: elementary, preparatory, and secondary. Education in government schools is free and is compulsory to age fourteen. Girls and boys go to separate schools. The UNRWA operates thirteen refugee camps in Jordan and offers education to refugee children, both boys and girls, in more than two hundred schools at the elementary and preparatory levels. There are several private schools administered by foreigners as well as by Jordanians; they are expensive and introduce Western curriculum along with core Jordanian curriculum. "Jordanian Society," a 1999 report by the Oslo-based Institute for Applied Social Science, stated that in attendance there was "little difference between boys and girls up to the Secondary School (level)" and that "77% of households have a basic school within a five to ten minutes walk" (*Jordan Times* 1998–99, 3). But while 92.6 percent of females attend elementary school, only 50.2 percent complete their secondary education and only one in five continues to the university (Hamdan 2000, 3).

Today, women make up the largest percentage of Jordan's university graduates. According to the curator of the Museum of Jordanian Heritage at Yarmouk University, between 1996 and 1998 women made up almost 80 percent of the student body at that university and comprised 90 percent of students at the Institute of Archeology and Anthropology, a traditional avenue of training for museum workers. These statistics have been attributed to the fact that women study harder than men and to the anticipation of jobs in the field as a benefit of peace with Israel (Hatamleh 1998a). Similarly high matriculation statistics for female students have been recorded at the University of Jordan in Amman.

Work

My advice to other women in the profession? Be meticulous.

—*Siham Balqar*

Is the education that women now have only a veneer under which women's traditional societal role remains unchanged? Will a woman's identifiers always be her family, her virginity, her marriage, her ability to bear sons, and her relationship with her mother-in-law?

Members of the royal family, in a balancing act between traditional and progressive, often become role models—setting standards and clarifying social issues. Mention has been made of Queen Rania's support of cultural activities; Basma, sister of the late King Hussein, works toward women's empowerment; Wijdan Ali, King Hussein's cousin, is an active professional and a leader in the arts; and Hussein's daughter, Lt. Col. Aisha, is not only a member of the armed forces but has been the head of the Directorate of Women's Affairs since 1995. Other role models in Amman who have influenced the development of museums are the wives and daughters of high government officials, including Sa'adieh Al Tel, Hind Nasser, Jane Mufti, and Samia Zaru, or the wives of prominent businessmen, including Suha Shoman and Widad Kawar.

Many educated women who work in Jordan's largest cities are aware of the dichotomy they, too, represent. They are spokespersons and perhaps role models for the goals of the kingdom and the modernization of the economy. Yet at the same time they are charged with the responsibility of upholding the moral and cultural values of society as child-bearers and symbols of traditional conservatism. This dual responsibility to themselves and other women, particularly the younger generation, can be stressful. It applies to royalty as well as to other classes. Hanan Al-Kurdi in Amman acknowledges this when she says, "Overall, women are confused now that they are 'outside the house' " (1999).

In England in 1998, speaking at a Lord Caradon Lecture on women and Islam, Princess Sarvath, wife of Prince Hassan, King Hussein's brother, proclaimed that Jordan's laws were conducive to women attaining a status in keeping with the essence of the religion and the aspirations of the leadership of the country. She confirmed that Islam "gave women the right to paid work, to own, inherit and bequeath property, and to learning . . . and that women are involved in many aspects of leadership in the country, they stand for election, serve in Parliament, hold responsible government positions and are actively involved in every sphere of life" (*Jordan Times* 1998–99, 5).

Women in Jordan can and do vote. Although Articles 6:22 and 23 of the Constitution provide for women's political, economic, and social equality, at one time Jordan's Electoral Law and Municipal Law denied women that right. The Electoral Law was amended in April 1974 and the Municipal Law in 1982, making women eligible to vote and run for office in national and municipal elections.

Before examining the place of women in the workforce, an overview of the major economic forces that have shaped modern Jordan's economy might be helpful. When Jordan annexed the West Bank and East Jerusalem in 1950, it more than doubled its population. After 1967, the Israeli occupation of the West Bank increased the Palestinian refugee population in Jordan, initially straining its resources and impeding development. Other forces impacting Jordan's economy were the civil war in Lebanon, the Jordanian civil war, the Gulf War, and Jordan's relationship with Israel.

By the 1970s, Jordan had begun investing in women's education and training, and there were skilled women to draw upon when many men left to work in the Gulf countries. As a result, in 1977, during King Hussein's silver jubilee, there was relative prosperity in the kingdom. The government, envisioning that Jordan could replace war-torn Beirut as the banking and service industry center in the region, began hiring women in many white-collar jobs (Layne 1994, xi). Women's employment was affected both by the migration of men to the oil-rich countries of the Persian Gulf and by the money the men sent back (Basson 1984). Although "the government actively promoted women's participation in the modern workforce through consciousness-raising seminars and legislation," this economic opportunity did not last, and "the trend toward more female participation . . . slowed by the mid 1980s due to recession . . . and the return of many male labor migrants" (Hijab 1988, 47).

After the signing of the 1979 Egyptian-Israeli peace treaty, Iraq and Kuwait became Jordan's leading trade partners. Economic conditions changed again after Iraq's 1990 invasion of Kuwait, however, resulting in a trade embargo and another influx of refugees from those countries. Since 2000, Jordan's economic potential is still being fed by change: a new king, peace with Israel, and new democratized attitudes toward its economy, privatization, and the press.

How do political events and economic boom-recessions affect women in the workforce? Shami, who has conducted research on the many forces at work on women in the labor force, concludes that the issue of employment in a society is interwoven with the role of women in that society and that the study of women's work should take into account the structure of the family, the domestic group, the kin group, and the nature of economic relations within these groups (Shami and Taminian 1990, xv).

As Chatty points out, an explosion of research and publications since 1990 demonstrates that women are seeking and finding ways to participate more fully in society. On the other hand, she acknowledges that governments and legislation are not reflecting or responding to this new initiative (2000, 241).

Improvement in women's economic status often requires that women be allowed to enter new work arenas and undertake new roles. Has this been true in Jordan? Economic development in the late twentieth century seems to have affected the middle and lower classes in Jordan differently. Women in both strata of society benefited from expanding educational opportunities, but while the overall shortage of professionals encouraged the employment of both male and female members of the middle class (Tucker 1988, 80), the kinds of work offered to women of the lower classes were limited. Often these women were relegated to jobs that kept them in the kitchens or in the traditional women's arenas of craft making, nurturing, or teaching other females. Several studies have shown how development favors men and often relegates women to noncompetitive areas. These women may freely participate, but only in the limited arenas designated as "women's professions." Middle-class women found better opportunities, less opposition to participation in the growing economy, and higher levels of acceptance by both their families and the public than did those of the lower classes (Quinn 1977, 185). Overall, women still constitute less than 16 percent of the labor force, and their average work period is approximately 3.7 years, compared with 44.8 years for men (Hamdan 2000, 3).

Amawi points out that women in the Jordanian workforce are "comparatively skilled and well educated. Of the Jordanian women who work outside the home, 46.4 percent are in professional or technical jobs. . . . Other data suggest that the smaller female workforce is much better educated and skilled than its male counterpart," adding that "legally . . . women enjoy equal protection with men under Jordanian labor law and civil service regulations" (Amawi 1996, 85).

In addition to their growing presence in civil service jobs, women are increasingly finding work in nongovernmental organizations (NGOs), such as women's organizations. Often such NGOs are formed for a single purpose and morph into many: the Queen Alia Foundation and the Noor Al Hussein Foundation, for example, support training and social programs and hire women to produce traditional arts and crafts. They offer a socially acceptable venue in which women may work, as well as an opportunity for volunteer participation. Volunteerism, however, has not been a tradition in

Jordanian museums. Indeed, this widespread tradition upon which American museums depend for their operation sets American museums apart from their counterparts in the rest of the world.

The age of women who successfully participate in the museum workforce today exhibits a pattern: older women are more successful and dynamic in achieving their goals. That might seem logical for the professional career woman in any society, but in Middle Eastern society there seems to be a general correlation between the amount of power a woman has and her age. While women in the workforce, married or not, are often given increased responsibility as they grow older, this does not reflect only the passage of time. For a married woman, some (but not all) of this personal accomplishment may relate to her identity as a wife and mother and to the success of her husband and sons. As for unmarried or older women holding administrative positions in the government or the private sector, they may not be perceived as a threat to the social or cultural integration of the country as long as they make symbolic concessions of behavior toward gender segregation and dress in the workplace.

Educated, unmarried, middle-class women after menopause experience less of a conflict between their personal choice of lifestyle or career and the restraints of religion or society (L. Abu-Lughod 1986). Norma Yessayan, a former office assistant at the National Gallery who once ran as a candidate for Parliament, pointed out that as an older woman she had no problems working with the male staff. "We never talked about the fact that I was a woman. I am older, so it's easier" (1999). Museum specialist Al-Kurdi (1999) likewise credited age as marking the point when people began to take her seriously.

Regardless of their education or position, all the women interviewed agreed that women in the Middle East live and work first and foremost as members of their own family. Within this family unit, most women are totally responsible for the care of children. But women in the workforce handle their child care and family responsibilities differently. When women's integration into the labor force was initially stated as a goal in the National Development Plan of 1975–80, women's education, special training programs, and child care centers were envisioned. A survey question posed about child care services within the Department of Antiquities showed no provisions at any museum site for such care. However, many women mentioned their maternity leave benefit of forty to sixty days and their understanding that child care service might now be under consideration at the Department of Antiquities in Amman.

At the Numismatic Museum of the Central Bank, two women who worked in collections management, both married with children, had different solutions to the problem of child care. Both worked from 7:45 in the morning until 4:00 in the afternoon, with Fridays and Saturdays off. Ghada Gordlow, a former inspector of currency at the bank, is Christian and a young mother of two. She has a maid to help with the children while she is at work. Her coworker, Rabiha Qorani, has four children, the youngest of whom is seven years old. She has no hired child care service. Dressing in a *hijab*, she balances her work and domestic responsibilities by rising early enough each morning to help her family off to school and then preparing their dinner before leaving home.

Many working women without domestic help find that astute planning, coupled with work hours that often end at 2:00 in the afternoon, allow them to continue traditional family schedules. Others count on the assistance of parents, grandparents, or other relatives to assist in child rearing. Members of traditionally close, multiaged family units act as a support net and participate in the domestic and child-rearing needs of the working mother.

Although her own children are grown, curator Muasar Audeh Hadidi in Salt is concerned about the need for child care programs for employees. She believes the issue should be on the agenda at the Department of Antiquities: "[It is] not yet, but it is one of our best goals" (Hadidi 1999). Administrator Ruba Abu Dalu in Irbid has two young children aged five and two, who are in a nearby school. If there are any problems, she counts on her mother to help. Curator Tamara Bermamet in Amman often counts on her mother-in-law: "It is more difficult for us [women], especially during the holidays, when we work. Where to put my children? The nursery school is closed, so I have to give my son to my mother-in-law" (1998).

For a balance between the traditional and the new, a few women, like Abu Dalu, believe that women must participate fully in society, and a way to do that is through women's organizations. She is one of four museum administrators who wear the *hijab*. "All women need more political and legal background . . . advice on how to transcend their traditional roles while maintaining the support of their families and community" (Abu Dalu 1998a).

Although women have won the right to work, they have not been relieved of social stereotypes or domestic responsibilities. It seems the fact that women were participating economically in their family's future had little effect on the expectations or demands of their families. Not only are women still expected to maintain domestic duties, but they also are assigned the role of representatives of tradition and national identity. They are under more pressure than men to conform to the rules of their social class, ethnic group, or religion. Moghadam explains that "gender politics are at the center of Islamist movements, where women assume the onerous burden of a largely male-defined tradition and are cast as the embodiment of cultural identity and the custodians of cultural values" (1994, 9).

But will inequality or repression continue when women are given equal opportunities for education and are well represented in the government, in civil service, at the universities, and in the armed forces? Time and again women in the workplace mentioned they were made examples of, and felt they had to be exemplary, even better than men. True, as women, they received equal pay. But what about the other aspects of their jobs, like opportunities for advancement or personal goal achievement? Khadijeh Quteishat, an administrator at the University of Jordan, makes clear her feelings about women's abilities, attitudes, and bias in an article in *Campus News* (1998, 3):

> Women are no less efficient than men and they can excel in any job assigned to them inasmuch as men can do, and they can even compete with men. . . . Nevertheless, and because of social factors that have denied women their potential, I feel that women should exert double the efforts needed by men to prove their social and professional equality with man. I feel that I still need to exert an extra effort to make them forget about the gender issue when they are talking business with me.

Saadawi discusses indicators of job equality in the broad Middle Eastern arena: "Women who are employed in government administration or elsewhere in the public sector are paid equal wages as compared to men. However, they are not afforded the same opportunities for promotion, or for appointment to responsible jobs or for training directed towards the preparation of employees for the higher positions" (1982, 187). Although women who work in museum-related government jobs in the Department of Antiquities insisted they receive equal pay, upon further discussion they revealed that men in their department whose wives do not work get fifteen Jordanian dinars more. Further, after a female employee's death, her children cannot receive her retirement pension. However, when a male retiree dies, a wife can receive his pension until her death, and their children can do so until they are eighteen (Naghawi and Qsoos 2000).

Many crosscurrents exist. In a discussion of equality in the workforce, Tamara Bermamet acknowledged equal pay and added that women get other kinds of benefits, including maternity leave, and: "Women can leave work one hour early to breast-feed their children—for up to one year." Asked what her male coworkers thought about this benefit, she answered: "They are happy they don't have to do that!" (Bermamet 1999).

Gendzier (1982, x) discredits the notion that modernization and development automatically improve the status of women. She argues that just as economic development is not identical with growth, neither is the increasing participation of women in the labor force in itself an automatic guarantee of improvement in her status.

While Jordan is a Muslim country, several different ethnic groups and religions coexist side by side. Jordan operates as an Islamic state, and public behavior is expected to conform to Islam. Islamic traditions dominate the activities of the populace. Women who do not conform publicly within the boundaries of proper dress, demeanor, or propriety are, at best, shunned.

Both ethnicity and religion were identifiable aspects among museum workers. Twenty-eight of the thirty-seven women who worked with Jordan's museums were Muslim; among those, four wore the *hijab*, and ten were Circassian. Circassians (both men and women) make up a large percentage of professionals in the museum workforce in proportion to the entire population. In his book on the history of the Circassians in Jordan, Haghandoqa states that traditionally "woman enjoys a high status among Circassians. They respect her, seek her advice" (1985, 70). Gallagher comments that Circassians are resented by some Jordanians for their prosperity, their preponderance in elite professions, and their Westernized outlook (1995, 223). The Circassian women in the museum workforce do support and network with each other, and, according to one arts administrator, "don't think others feel prejudice against them" (Mufti 1999).

Nine of the thirty-seven women were Christian. Two, who did not wish to be quoted, felt that Islam restricted them. They felt they had to conform to the Muslim way of life publicly, and their career opportunities may have been hindered because they were a minority. However, they claimed their professional relationships with Muslim women in the museum arena were religion-blind.

To many of the women interviewed in government museums, the issue of individuality—the focus on personal satisfaction—was an unaccustomed goal and an uncomfortable one. Individuality is sometimes thought of as an indulgent Western goal or a form of narcissism, whereas "identity" for them is contained in the collective selfhood found in their society through kinship ties and the extended family. "Individuality" is also often equated with more responsibility. Curators revealed this in many ways. For instance, questions about career goals were often answered by collective ways to better their department or were directed toward the needs of their peers. In Amman, for example, Lubna Hashem was comfortable as a team member "dedicated to the concept of her virtual museum and wanted more than anything to make it work" (1999). Although many respondents actually held no power over long-range policies or decisions, they felt heavy responsibility for the day-to-day success of museum operation, often recognizing that advancement meant involvement in the male world of politics and bureaucracy, areas that they were not trained for.

Dealing as it did with educated women of the middle and upper classes, this research involved some women who acknowledged they had already achieved their professional aspirations. Perhaps this is so because they could compare it to the past, when there were no such career opportunities. Progress is comparative and situational; so is perspective. To these women, professional inequality and gender bias seemed to be outside their area of concern. In one case, a curator felt that "being a woman was a plus. I never felt discriminated against. We were protected . . . even when we [archeologists] went out in the desert. But with other women, we were competitive" (Al-Kurdi 1999).

The fact that they and some others had achieved so much blinded them to the goal of equality for all women. This can be illustrated by the paucity of networking or mentoring activities, and is perhaps best summed up by Rula Qsoos at the Department of Antiquities: "We have no time to change the world" (Qsoos 2000). Mentoring activities were at best subtle both between women and men and between women and women. Two female administrators admitted they preferred hiring men: Zahida Safer (1998) at the Central Bank and Suha Shoman (1999) at the Darat al Funun. Both explained that women leave jobs more often than men do because of personal or family reasons, and employers see this as a loss of invested time and training.

What kinds of support did women curators receive in pursuing their education and in their museum work? Although several women gave credit to their mothers for being an inspiration, only two curators, Hanan Al-Kurdi (1999) and Arwa Masaadeh (1999), admitted to having nonfamily mentors, both of whom were men. Eman Oweis in Jerash and Sawsan Al-Fakhri in Aqaba mentioned that their fathers supported their decisions for higher education and choice of profession. Al-Fakhri's mother thought it would be too hot under the sun for her daughter to have a career in archeology, but her father prevailed. When discussion of the *hijab* she was wearing came up, she was quick to state that it had many advantages: "Even the men cover their heads against the sun in this climate" (Al-Fakhri 1999). Oweis (1999a) also credits her husband for his support of her career. Arwa Masaadeh, one of the youngest curators, gives credit to her director, Dr. Bisheh, for his support. "I felt strange, I was a girl, unmarried. I had to prove myself. My director said I would be good at the job—to phone him if I needed help—and a couple of times when the men here didn't like what I planned I called him and he backed me up" (Masaadeh 1999). She also had the unwavering support of her parents. Since 1983 her mother, Fowzia Zayyaden, has worked in various jobs at the Kerak museums. She had no formal schooling after secondary school, and bore eight children. When they grew up, she went to work. Her husband insisted that all the children get an education, even the girls. "My husband worked at the museum in the morning, me in the afternoon. He died six years ago. All my children are getting an education. I must work to get education for my kids. I've asked myself why I suffered with a big family—two or three are enough in these hard times. Nowadays, girls must have education for the future—if she doesn't marry, she has to take care of herself" (Zayyaden 1999).

Feminism

I don't belong to any women's organizations—I belong to myself.

—*Aida Naghawi*

The women interviewed were often ambivalent and divided over the issue of women's rights; some denied there was a need to change the existing status of women because Islam provides for their equality and identity. A few others claimed that feminism represented the continuation of colonialism and that the issue was entirely a Western phenomenon. Some even denied the need for women's rights organizations, citing their own accomplishments and perceived freedom. But many others supported the existing women's organizations that work in Jordan for social change and gender equality.

An important question involving gender issues that Jordanian women face is whose standards and tactics to use to help promote change. They could use the West as an example, with all its inappropriateness, or they could use Islam as a guideline. But if they chose the latter, according to Kandiyoti, identification with Islam's cultural authenticity meant they had two choices: denying that Islamic practices were necessarily oppressive or asserting that oppressive practices were not necessarily Islamic (Kandiyoti 1996, 9). Some women doubted the relevancy of Western feminist agendas for them. "What issues should we care about? Wearing shorts?" asked Samia Zaru (1999). The angry rhetoric and media exposure of bra burning in the United States is decades old yet remains a representative image of the Western women's movement. Many Jordanian women regard the aggressive negativism of the Western women's liberation movements as not only embarrassing but counterproductive to achieving the changes they wish for in their own society. For instance, Hanan Al-Kurdi believes in "positive, passive, resistance . . . like Ghandi . . . for women's issues" (1999).

Jordan's feminist movement is not as old as Egypt's, which began in the late nineteenth century and has been almost exclusively the province of middle- and upper-class women. Tucker asserts that the Egyptian women's movement can serve to illustrate the narrow base and vision of feminism in the region (1988, 38). Could it be that only the strong and the wealthy can effectively direct their own destinies?

Chatty points out that governments in the Middle East display a continued reluctance to allow women to come together in formal groups (2000, 241). Women's unions and societies do exist in Jordan, but most were originally created, organized, and controlled by men. Although now some really are administered by women, in others women still serve only as figureheads.

Women's rights organizations in Jordan are affiliated closely with the state, not only because they need government permission to operate but also because the government has initiated and controlled most of them.

This relationship may make them less strident in their approach to reform, but it also helps protect them from public censure and serious backlash from those opposed to liberalization. Ramadan mentions early support in the 1970s by Queen Zain Al Sharaf: "Under Her Majesty's leadership and benevolent guidance many of Jordan's women took the initiative to participate and play a bigger role in the fields of charity and social welfare" (n.d., 52).

The first of these women's organizations in Jordan were charitable. In 1944 the United Women's Social Organization was founded, followed in 1945 by the Organization of United Jordanian Women. In 1949 the two merged to form the government-sponsored Jordan Women's Hashemite Union, which was dissolved that same year. In 1971 the Arab Women Organization was established, and the government founded the Women's Federation. In 1981 the Women's Federation was dissolved, to be replaced by the Jordanian Women's Union, which was in turn dissolved by the government in 1989.

Today, several women's organizations operate in Jordan. One of the most influential is the 120,000-member Jordanian National Forum for Women (JNFW). A grassroots organization, it works on the community level, acting as a support group and lobbyist for women seeking election to local municipal councils. It is governed by a support group and higher council chaired by HRH Princess Basma bint Talal. Another women's group is the Jordanian National Committee for Women (JNCW), which focuses on government policy. Basma bint Talal is the president of this elite organization, which is hosted by the Queen Alia Fund for Social Development. Still another influential women's group is the Jordanian Women's Union (JWU), formed to increase awareness of women's rights under national laws. Established in 1945, it was dissolved twice, in 1975 and 1981, then reorganized in 1987. It now claims three thousand members and is headed by Amneh Al Zoubi ("Feminist Movement Rewriting 'His Story' " 1999).

Several other organizations also exist to support women. Among them are the Princess Basma Women's Resource Center, which acts as a resource for policymakers and women's groups, collects data, and conducts training courses; the al-Kutba Institute for Human Development, which assists in community development; and the Center of Woman's Studies, which provides information on women's issues.

Eman Oweis (1999b) and Ruba Abu Dalu (1998b) were two curator/ administrators actively participating in local women's organizations. It is interesting to note that both women are from smaller cities in Jordan. Abu Dalu belongs to the Irbid chapter of the General Federation of Jordanian Women. Oweis belongs to the Jerash Women's Association, an organization that helps needy women in villages by providing information about health, birth control, and education.

Women and Museum Work

Someone once aptly said, "Jordan is a museum both above and below the ground."
—Hussein Ibn Talal

The Purpose of Museums

Museums mean different things to different people. Museums satisfy differing needs and espouse different purposes. How do they serve, empower, advance, and educate society in general—and women in particular? To some people, the very word connotes age and authority, stuffiness and boredom; to others it means excellence, preservation, education, and fun. To governments, museums are not so ambiguous or vague: museums become the representative of the government and are often vehicles for social control.

In the United States a common public perception is that museums are either dusty repositories of objects made by dead white men, or places of recreation that might provide an afternoon's diversion or entertainment. The American museum educator John Cotton Dana attempted a definition: "The word museum will long continue to arouse in the minds of most the thought of ancient, rare, curious and beautiful things" (1917, 29). A more contemporary definition, by museum educator Flora Kaplan, describes museums as "spaces in which elites and competing social groups express their ideas and world views" (1994, 2).

Like many institutions, museums have sought to develop a life of their own—to promote, institutionalize, and evaluate their own existence. The result has been a search for a universal definition.

According to the American Association of Museums (AAM), a museum is "an organized and permanent nonprofit institution, essentially educational or esthetic or with a purpose, with a professional staff, which owns

22

and utilizes tangible objects, cares for them, and exhibits them to the public on some regular schedule" (Fitzgerald 1973, 8).

Most of the museums in Jordan are members of the International Council of Museums (ICOM), which provides a similar definition for the term *museum:* "a non-profit-making, permanent institution in the service of society and of its development, and open to the public, which acquires, conserves, researches, communicates, and exhibits, for purposes of study, education and enjoyment, material evidence of people and their environment" (ICOM 1974).

These definitions support the legitimacy of museums and what they should do, but not how or why they should exist. My research investigated practicality: What do museums do? What are they for? Some answers included: "They give you nostalgia for the past." And also: "They give to people what they want to present of themselves." Obviously museum exhibitions are editorial. They do more than report, catalog, or present. They also argue, compare, discover, investigate, and propagandize. What makes a great museum exhibition memorable to us, whether it is of contemporary painting or Umayyad pottery, is not its dispassionate presentation of facts or the objective skill with which curators describe or document some particular historical or artistic movement. What makes an exhibit memorable is its capacity to move us, to provide us with fresh insights, and to induce in us a sense of enlightenment, understanding, or transformation.

Because one cannot consider objects in museums without considering the social context of their past, present, and future, museums become institutions of identity: concerned with the who, what, where, when, and why of objects that identify the maker and the culture. This implies dealing in practicalities and specifics, not philosophical inquiry. Yet museums, through their commitment to museological systems, develop their own theoretical framework, and this is achieved regardless of the differing opinions as to whether museology belongs with the applied sciences or is a scientific discipline.

Usually, museums interpret the significance of objects and explain them in an educational format using standardized techniques that include reproductions, transfers, restorations, photographic or laser imagery, and the spoken or written word as well as the display of original objects. Jordan's museums use all these techniques in their exhibitions.

To be certain that my definition of a museum, based on the AAM's guidelines, was not confusing or distorting my research by predetermined concepts from twenty-three years of museum work in the United States, I needed to know what the definition and purpose of a museum were to museum personnel in Jordan. In later discussion, my inquiry was expanded to determine to what extent their comments mirrored the actual operations and activities of their institutions.

The definition of museums varied. Both definitions and purposes swung from grave reverence to flippancy and across a spectrum of meanings (Rishaidat 1994, 175–82).

In the search for common ground, inquiry began with the formal and progressed to the personal. The *Dictionary of the Arab Language* defines a museum as "the place of artistic things; new and ancient things, or the house or place in which you put beautiful art" (Mitri 1979, 136).

Traditional Jordanian definitions of "museum" include such statements as "Museums are institutions serving the three main functions of collecting, preservation and presentation of objects" (M. Zaru 1996, 1), and "Museums are the result of an effort dedicated to protect mankind's heritage for generations to come" (Bisharat 1994, 159). In 1994, the curator of the Jordan Archeological Museum, Siham Balqar, defined museums as centers of significant collections of objects and materials essential to the study of the humanities. "They serve the public not only through exhibitions and other programs but also through the preservation of the primary resources of the country's heritage and the maintenance and organization of the museum's collections" (1994, 155).

In 1998, Ghazi Bisheh, director general of the Department of Antiquities, addressed the purpose and the ownership of museums in Jordan: "A museum shouldn't just be for the exhibit of artifacts. Basically it is an education center where the local community comes to learn, interact. It organizes and promotes activities, especially for kids. Then they themselves will start to protect their heritage. It belongs to them . . . not the government . . . it belongs to them" (Bisheh 1999).

Museum Work

A museum is an encapsulation of history.

—*Ibrahim Abu-Lughod*

In the 1990s in the Middle East, taboos still prevailed concerning the public mixing of the sexes, and women still preferred certain professions. Female university graduates in the workforce in Jordan were most often employed as teachers in girls' schools, as professors in women's faculties, and as doctors—usually gynecologists and pediatricians. Those with less education often chose work as nurses in women's and children's hospital wards. These professions have a history of acceptance in the Middle East. Expanded interest in museum work began during the 1990s, and there was also a rise in curatorial appointments to government museums.

How is museum work defined? What is museum work? What is the job description and what are the actual responsibilities of museum curators and administrators in government museums? When envisioned in Western terms, job descriptions of administrators and curators are usually separate, and the responsibilities differ. Both positions involve scholarship and connoisseurship, a great deal of public contact, writing, managerial skills, data management, and specific academic training. Most private, government, and university museums in the United States also require participation from staff in public relations, publications, and fundraising.

Two examples from *Aviso* (1999, 7), the monthly job-listing newsletter of the AAM, speak to the typical responsibilities of curators:

Duties include supervision of department's associate curator and administrative staff and responsibility for acquisitions, cataloging, publications, exhibitions and care of collections. . . . Seeking a dynamic individual to handle the research, documentation, exhibit preparation, interpretation, and development of its Egyptian and Mesopotamian collection . . . This includes maintenance and supervision of artifact storage, cataloging and packing and shipping of artifacts.

Provides guidance and direction for department's growth and plans accordingly. Supervises access to collections, provides care and conservation of artifacts, and monitors environmental conditions. Leads team in planning and managing current and future exhibits.

How do the duties outlined in the above job postings compare with the actual work situations in Jordan's museums? Do the responsibilities of their government-employed curators differ? Are there similarities between the positions in art, history, and private or university museums?

Before citing specific data and comparisons, perhaps a comment on both the organizational structure of professional museum work and women's participation in it will help illustrate the present situation. As mentioned earlier, the three employment situations most viable for Jordan's university archeology graduates were work in the Department of Archeology, fieldwork, and work in museums (Bermamet 1998).

Although many of the women curators interviewed offered an oral description of their duties, none provided documentation or specifics. One former curator recounted, however, that "there is no organizational structure, no job descriptions—we [in the Department] wrote a policy because we didn't know what our job was" (Al-Kurdi 1999).

The research questionnaire requested acknowledgment of responsibilities in the following areas: administration, research, curating of exhibits, collections management, public relations, teaching, grant writing, and tour guiding. Six curators provided the following written information about their job responsibilities:

Administrative 4
Research 4
Curating/collection management 6
Public relations 4
Teaching 1
Grantsmanship 0
Tour guiding 2
Publications 3

Thirteen others verbally described their responsibilities:

Administration 9
Research 5
Curating, collections management 13
Public relations 4
Teaching 3
Grantsmanship 2

Tour guiding 8
Publications 4

Unlike the distinct separation between director and curator in the United States, in Jordan the job of curator involves administration of the site. Often the position includes research in the field and some public relations but usually not teaching, grantsmanship, or giving school tours. The private museums defined jobs more clearly, aware of the separation between the director's position and that of curatorial staff.

What is the range of activities in both government and private museums in Jordan? All thirty-six museums (except the virtual Museum With No Frontiers) offered displays of original, tangible objects. The next most prevalent activity in museums was lectures (fifteen), followed by classes (nine), musical performances (five), dance or festivals (three), theater (two), and poetry readings (one). The private art institutions (the Jordan National Gallery, the Haya Cultural Center, and the Darat al Funun) held the broadest range of activities, incorporating all types of events into their schedules. Those governed by the Waqf, the Islamic Museum at the King Abdullah Mosque, and the Mazar Islamic Museum in Kerak, offered the least number of cultural activities to the public.

Museology Training

Yes, I want to get my master's degree, but I have children, my work, and my home.
—*Manal Awamleh*

For museum personnel, training in museology is often an afterthought. Most of the present curators and administrators in Jordan's museums have only had exposure to museology through a core course taught for one semester as part of the degree in archeology at the University of Jordan. The course focuses heavily on exhibit design but also includes early technology, conservation of materials, and museology. A detailed description of the course appears in appendix B. Curator Huda Kilani described her class project as a report on a "model museum" that included analysis of proper storage, lighting, color, and exhibit design.

Several other curators augmented their studies through the occasional seminars and workshops in museum studies sponsored by Yarmouk University and the University of Jordan. In addition, the Ford Foundation funded a series of museological training workshops at the Jordan National Gallery in 1990 for museum personnel and Department of Antiquities curatorial staff. These workshops were Jordan's first shared experience in museology. Lecturers from the Smithsonian Institution and the Metropolitan Museum presented programs on documentation systems, exhibition techniques, storage, conservation, registration, labeling, and education activities. In the past, the Jordan Archeological Museum in Amman participated in an exchange of museum personnel with Harvard University through the International Partners among Museums (IPAM) program, sending Siham Balqar to study at the Semitic Museum. Nazmieh Rida Tawfiq Darwish studied museology and national park management through a USAID graduate school scholarship to the United States. But opportunities such as these have been few. Most often, when the Department of Antiquities has given curators the opportunity to continue their studies, it has been in the area of conservation and restoration.

Before assuming full responsibilities at their institution, few curators or administrators had opportunities to learn about museum and collections management from their mentors, or to work as assistants on the job. However, Huda Kilani had such an opportunity with Sa'adieh Al Tel at the Museum of Popular Traditions. Others, like Wijdan Ali and Suha Shoman, made full use of books, travel, and professional networking to set up effective museological procedures and goals at their institutions.

In a 1998 issue of *Campus News*, citing career development at the University of Jordan, Nabil Khairy announced plans for the establishment of a doctoral program in archeology and a reorganization that would convert the Department of Archeology into an archeology institute. More important for museum training, he indicated that the Institute of Archeology and Anthropology at Yarmouk University intended to establish a department of museology that would promote "archeological research, field activities and administrative MA programmes" (1998, 13).

As Jordan considers construction of seven new museums, Hind Nasser argues for the immediate need for trained museum personnel. Speaking about the National Museum: "We did the plan, but who would run such a museum? We even thought of sending people on scholarships abroad. We should teach [museology] here for the whole Middle East! Nobody has started it!" (1999).

Education Programs

The relationship between schools and museums can be called promising or problematic, depending on whom you talk to in Jordan. At the Jordan National Gallery, Wijdan Ali believes that for young people, education in the arts should be a high priority. From the beginning, workshops and tours for students have been important program objectives there. Ruba Abu Dalu in Irbid stressed that their new museum would contain an educational center that would create outreach programs for school children. Nazmieh Rida Tawfiq Darwish at the Department of Antiquities confirmed that "school trips to archeological museums are among the most important extra-curricular activities. . . . They also play a vital part in achieving some of the objectives of the Department . . . in its role as the government agency responsible for museums" (1994, 183).

In a speech to ICOM, Hardoy paints a dark but common picture of the educational activities many museums offer: "Pupils and teachers are frequently visitors to museums but this does not mean that they understand what they go there to see. . . . Schoolchildren thus become museum visitors attending under compulsion by virtue of their country's education programme" (1986, 14).

In Jordan the present curriculum for schools includes a museum visitation component, according to art educator Samia Zaru. However, the reality is that these visits are not always carried out, or the time allocated is sometimes used for other, in-house activities. A plethora of factors contribute to this situation, including funding, scheduling coordination, transportation, the weather and timing (no visitations during Ramadan or the rainy season), and teacher training.

Museum curators at the government museums in Amman confirmed that the public schools were scheduled for visits on a regular basis and that the teachers who accompanied them were responsible for the guided tours. Educational tours were based on information provided by the Department of Antiquities because the museums themselves had no education department or education specialists. There were, however, exceptions to this. Some curators and administrators in Madaba, Irbid, and Jerash took a personal hands-on approach to education—occasionally guiding groups themselves—and regularly going into the schools with programs they had developed about their sites and collections.

Notably, two women have been active in educational training and curriculum development: Margo Meltligian, who is credited as the first Jordanian woman to start museum programs in schools, and Samia Zaru, who recently completed a series of videos for young students on art education that explored artistic creation, color, form, shape, and design. One of these videos featured the Jordan National Gallery and the Darat al Funun, where young people participated in guided tours and experienced the dynamics of visual creativity in the museum settings.

Although docenting as it is practiced in museums in the United States does not exist in Jordan, several private museums offer guided tours on a scheduled basis by trained staff and volunteers. Tours are available by appointment at the Haya Science Museum, the Jordan National Gallery, the Darat al Funun, and the Numismatic Museum of the Central Bank. Most school visits to museums are free to students; however, at the Haya Science Museum, where grades three through twelve visit twice a semester, there is a charge of one-half a Jordanian dinar per child.

Three innovative programs that attempt to bring students and museums together through educational programming are those of the Ahliyyah School for Girls (ASG), the Friends of Archeology, and the Awareness Program for children through the Department of Antiquities. At the ASG, students in the Archeological Club, which was founded in 1996, visit museums, interview archeologists, and actually go on digs. Headed by Khawla Goussous, an archeologist formerly with the Department of Antiquities, the club's activities are comprehensive.

The second program, created by the Friends of Archeology in 1999 for young people, is the school membership program, dedicated to promoting appreciation and knowledge of Jordan's antiquities. Schools that join have access to research facilities and scholars attached to institutions such as the American Center for Oriental Research.

The third program, developed by the Department of Antiquities, offers children the opportunity to do excavations in the summer. Nazmieh Rida Tawfiq Darwish also created an innovative museum program in 1979 wherein students could visit archeological sites on Fridays, their day off, learn about the antiquities, and help clean the grounds. Free transportation, Pepsi, and food were provided.

Officials at the Department of Antiquities have been concerned with the trashing of antiquities sites by school groups and wonder about the actual amount of learning going on. Children on these visits need a great deal of supervision, and the sites are extensive. Through the use of questionnaires, the department has explored the effectiveness of these museum visits. The results of their research, published in 1994, cited lack of comprehensive planning and ambiguous objectives. Further, the research found teachers were limited in their knowledge of the sites and many believed the purpose of these visits was entertainment. Eight suggestions for improvement in the visitation program were offered, including adding archeology studies and art history to school curriculum, improving training programs, providing better access to books and related materials and translating existing ones into Arabic, drawing more media attention to the issue, and augmenting the in-school programs to use professionally trained department staff (Darwish 1994, 184–85).

National Heritage

> Jordan is an open museum. In Jordan, one experiences the ecstasy of eternity!
> —*Hasan Ayed*

How much did Jordan's antiquity or its colonial heritage influence the present-day establishment and operation of its museums? How does the search for cultural identity (*al-hawia al-kawmia)* or national heritage *(turath)* play a role in the establishment of museums and the presentation of programs and exhibits? In a country where politics is linked closely to land and tradition, are museums staging grounds for the development of democratic principles, or do they reflect the decadent excess of continued Western hegemony? Are museums attempting to validate the importance of Jordan as a reaction to Israeli archeological interpretations, or to rhetoric by Israeli politicians such as Ariel Sharon who claim that Jordan is actually Palestine? Is it the government's agenda to foster unification and promote national pride in this country so recently created with its diverse peoples, political uncertainties, and continuing influx of emigrating populations? These issues may be the most important reasons for building museums.

In contrast to official national policy, are minority groups in Jordan building museums? Do the agendas of minority groups within Jordan include the establishment of private museums dedicated to ensure separation and the preservation of their ethnic individuality? If so, are the two agendas compatible?

These questions surface when one investigates the purpose of Jordan's museums. If they are being developed to promote historic continuity and cultural identity with the ancient dwellers of the area, might that mean a close identification with non-Arabs, therefore impeding governmental nationalist aspirations? Jordan identifies with many cultures, periods, and traditions. How should the museums reflect this? Whose history and whose way of life should be promoted in Jordan's museums: the invaders from the East or the West, the Muslim, the Bedouin, the Palestinian? Is there a conflict here with nation building?

A nation often seeks its validity from the traditions of its past—from culture or cultures that came before. Historical continuity that is developed from this evidence legitimizes the present inhabitants of a site. The search to identify and promote collective national heritage in the twentieth century has been manifested differently in each country in the Middle East. The extensive archeological and architectural ruins are the most obvious testimony of Jordan's history.

Throughout the Middle East, preoccupation with the idea of "nation," independence from European rulers, and the development of national movements has been linked directly to the establishment of museums. Egyptian museums took the lead in fostering a sense of cultural continuity through their presentations. Discoveries of ancient civilizations gave legitimacy to the creation of museums, which then sought to appeal to the memory of a pre-Islamic past.

Early in the last century, the Egyptians began to develop their ideology and literature and to legitimize their historical continuity through the arts. Iraq attempted to do the same a few decades later. The wealth and organization of these neighbors overshadowed Jordan, which had fewer resources and less famous antiquities than those of Pharaonic, Assyrian, or Babylonian origin. Instead of identifying solely with an ancient heritage based on the Nabataean culture at Petra, Jordan has focused its collective memory on more recent events, specifically the Arab Revolt of 1916–18 and the Hashemite participation in it. Its "nationhood" has been problematic because of the circumstances of its creation and its relationships with Palestine and Israel. These relationships, however, help to define Jordan today.

Cultural Identity

Museums and the objects they display, protect, and study have become valuable tools in the promotion of cultural identity and the application of national cultural policies. "Museums allow the visual discovery of the ancient or modern history of a people or a nation, not only at the level of systematic intellectual knowledge . . . but also at the deepest and most subtle level, that of sensitivity and emotion, which directly strikes the social consciousness" (Abranches 1983, 19–20).

The issue of cultural identity was stressed at the 1994 ICOM Encounter in Amman. Participants addressed the importance of the role of museums in society, charging that the first task of Arab museums is the protection of the national and human heritage and the "valorization of the concept of a cultural identity in all present and future museums" (ICOM 1994, 37). Maffi, in her discussion of the manipulation of history in service to Jordanian cultural identity, observed that museums are key places that allow the "monitoring of the evolution of the official representation of history that is given by the political power" (1999, 85).

Museums can be the meeting place, the melting pot of different peoples, and a place where citizens can become unified. Jordan represents a complex, changing model for categorizing cultural identity. Museums help establish the connections and historical continuity through their exhibitions, publications, and programs. For example, Maffi describes how the museum exhibition at Yarmouk University promotes the central theme of the importance of Jordan (Jund al-Urdun) as a "regional linchpin" in economic, urban, and cultural development. There the viewer is led to the conclusion that the Umayyads were the creators of the Arabic name of Jordan: they first used the term *Urdun*, from which the present name of the country is derived (Maffi 1999, 95).

This shaping of cultural identity is apparent in other ways. Little didactic reference to the British Mandate period is found in Jordan's museums. If objects from that period are displayed at all, they are situational, in the context of the seamlessness of Arab and Bedouin continuity. This apparent marginalization or denial of the colonial period is an attempt to promote the continuity of Jordanian identity; given that King Abdullah's mother was British, it will be interesting to watch future developments in this area. Could reaction to the colonialist period also have been a factor in the deaccessioning of the Orientalist collection at the Jordan National Gallery?

But reference to and representation of the Ottoman and Mandate periods is not completely absent in Jordan's museums. It exists in presentations at the Martyr's Memorial, where war materiel and memorabilia interpret the Jordanian role in the Arab Revolt, and in the contemporary history museums that feature objects owned by the Hashemite family during those eras. Period furniture settings are another area of identification, as are illuminated documents in the folklore museums throughout the country, in the Islamic and Sharif Hussein Bin Ali Museums, and in the Numismatic and Stamp Museums of Amman.

This disassociation is not complete; Jordan attempts to perpetuate its image as a part of the exotic Middle East—continuing to market and identify itself visually with an Orientalist past. This image, calculated to increase cultural tourism and build an identity, both within Jordan and internationally, capitalizes on the noble honor and strength of the Bedouin. It has other implications besides cultural tourism and identity building externally and internally, and can send other signals that reinforce a subservient role for women. It is this image of the Bedouin that is promoted to represent Jordan publicly abroad in its advertising and public relations campaigns. Several scholars, including Brand, have explored the gender issues of nationalism and the development of cultural identity in Jordan.

Layne suggests four areas of national identification that are promoted by the Jordanian government: first, Jordan's tribal heritage, which has been expropriated by the state as a symbol of national identity; second, Jordan's role in the revolt against the Ottomans; third, the Hashemite descent from the Prophet; and fourth, the distinctiveness of Jordan "vis-à-vis its most significant other, Palestine" (1994, 102–3).

Kaplan points out that museums emerged in Western democratic nation-states and seem to thrive best in democracies (1994, 2). She also asserts that scientific advancement and the rise of capitalism in the West, along with industrialization and the end of colonialism, helped to instigate and promote the establishment of museums in the twentieth century (1994, 2). Hardoy argues along similar lines, asserting that museums, as places for collective thought, analysis, and discussion, present the most direct path to development for a country and the most direct support that can be given to a democracy (1986, 17).

The importance of developing cultural identity in Jordan is demonstrated by proceedings at the 1994 Arab-ICOM meeting in Amman: "The recent upsurge in interest in museums throughout much of the Arab world comes from a new sense of defining and transmitting one's identity" (Bisharat 1994, 160). Can museums promote a cohesive cultural identity and at the same time reflect diversity in emerging democratic societies?

Abranches believes that they can "if one envisions this nationalism as a form of social conscience that commits a group of people to understand and accept each other, and above all, to communicate positively, intellectually, and spiritually under the shelter of a state political structure and on the basis of common economic and social activities, even if their cultural specifics remain" (1983, 225).

However, the concept that museums should foster patriotism or purposefully shape cultural identity is not universally accepted. Some abhor it, arguing that museums should be above political agendas or constituency promotion and should exist solely in service to truth and enlightenment. Hans van Dijk writes: "The representations of the culture of a society are no more than portraits of the era, never a society's 'cultural identity' for a 'cultural identity' is a figment of the imagination of nationalists and racists" (1993, 42).

Still others feel it should be the role of museums to create and perpetuate nationalism and cultural identity. This view is implicit in Hernan Crespo's comments at the ICOM 89 conference: "Our population are subjected to a permanent process of estrangement when, by means of the media, we are invaded by foreign examples, anti-values which threaten our specific characteristics. It is thus that, in many cases, language is deformed or denatured as well as are religious beliefs, celebrations, dress, even ways of life" (1989, 30).

How are Jordan's museums used to create, manipulate, and disseminate the concepts of national heritage and cultural identity? Presently Jordan has eight museums of modern history (including the Stamp Museum and the Numismatic Museum at the Central Bank) that are dedicated to presenting the story of the Hashemite dynasty. Their focus is the historical pan-Arab role of the Hashemites, the iconization of the Bedouin, and articulation of the direct connection between the present and ancient civilizations that have inhabited the area. These museums also help to confer legitimacy on the Hashemites by presenting religious connections that stress their direct descent from the prophet Muhammad. An example of this is the Islamic Museum, located in the King Abdullah Mosque in Amman, which features the personal effects of King Abdullah I along with objects from ancient sites. Several museums specifically dramatize the role of the Hashemites in the Great Arab Revolt—their leadership in the victory over the Ottomans, their fight for independence, and their subsequent legitimization as the rulers of Jordan. These include the Sharif Hussein Bin Ali Museum at Raghdan Palace, the Martyrs Memorial, and the future Museum of Political History in Amman, as well as the King Abdullah Museum in Ma'an.

In addition to Hashemite legitimacy, historically Jordan has also defined itself through its relationship to Palestine. After the creation of Israel in 1948 and again after the loss of the West Bank in 1967, the influx of refugees from Palestine so changed the demographics of Jordan that Palestinians became a majority. Initially, Jordanian and Palestinian art and artifact (particularly women's costume) were promoted together in the folkloric museums built in the 1970s. Exhibits fostered a common identity through the side-by-side presentation of cultural items and discussion of iconography. Leading the development of this unification was the Museum of Popular Traditions, founded in 1971 in Amman.

Political changes again manifested themselves in Jordan's museums in the late 1970s. The civil war between the Palestinians and the Jordanians threatened to undermine the stability of the country. This tension was reflected in Jordan's museums: Palestinian cultural representation lessened and the Bedouin, as the Jordanian cultural symbol, was given greater prominence, taking precedence over the crafts and costume of the villager. This committed refocus on the separateness of Jordanians and Palestinians meant museum idealization of Bedouin life and reassertion of the role of the Hashemites as the legitimate cultural representatives of the country. Such examples of Bedouin life and their tent environment can be seen in the National Heritage Museum at the University of Jordan and the Salt Folklore Museum.

Maffi calls the creation of this new staged and blended nationalist culture "folklorization" (1999, 90). Arising from the need to invent new and comprehensive origins and build a legitimizing past while also building an imaginary community with legitimacy in the real world, this process transformed Jordan into a common synthesis of a timeless world, deprived of its historical and spatial dimension.

Creating a culture or shaping it is not an easy task. Not only are ethnic, political, and nationalist issues involved, but gender and identity issues as well. Museums can be places of comfort or places of change. People can find comfort in the continuity of their history—or confusion. What people see in a museum, what is preserved from the past and on view in the present, will influence tomorrow. What a museum chooses to collect and exhibit and how it goes about that job reflects the point of view of the leadership.

Silent messages about identity and continuity were evident to Layne. Her insight into the purpose of the exhibit she visited in 1981 at the Krayma Community Center in the Jordan Valley makes this point. Looking at the collection of mostly utilitarian objects on display, she recognized them all—and the labels reinforced their identity. But the exhibit contained no contextual information such as provenance, manufacture, or specific use. All of this was already self-evident to the audience. Only later did she recognize the importance of that message and the reason for the existence of the exhibit: "It was clearly an exhibition of themselves to themselves" (Layne 1994, 133).

Display itself sends silent messages about power, identity, and continuity. Exhibits in folkloric or ethnographic museums such as the museum in Salt, Amman's Folklore Museum, and the university's National Heritage Museum that show women engaged at work in weaving, cooking, and grinding—and men at leisure smoking, lounging on pillows, or drinking coffee—reinforce the inequality of women and perpetuate traditional stereotypes.

How do the museums in Jordan reflect government leadership and policy, compared with the museums of its Arab neighbors? Stephen Weil observes that a museum's goal of universal understanding may be desired but impossible: "In a world of conflicting interests, a museum that serves one community beneficially may, when considered from the perspective of another, appear to be anything but benign" (1997, 53). For example, Weil continues, a military museum in Iraq during Saddam Hussein's rule might have included activities contrary to museum operation definitions set by UNESCO or ICOM. According to refugees with whom I spoke, public art in Saddam Hussein's Iraq reflected the taste and directives of the government—at the art schools, museums, and outside in public art projects.

Iraq is a good example of government policy and its relationship to the arts. It has historic ties with Jordan: members of the Hashemite dynasty were assassinated in Iraq; Iraq has been a major trading partner; and it has influenced Jordan in many areas, including the cultural arena. How have the great shifts in policy and regime since 1989 affected the once-lauded National Museum in Baghdad? After Iraq's invasion of Kuwait, the museum first received and then returned Kuwaiti museum treasures; nearby bombing in early 1991, during the first gulf war, and extensive looting in April 2003, during the second gulf war, resulted in the loss, damage, or destruction of a large proportion of its artifacts. These events were devastating to museum professionals.

One can compare the differences in government policy regarding public art between the late King Hussein of Jordan and former President Saddam Hussein of Iraq through two public sculpture projects. In Amman the striking but passive sculpture by Rami Bsharat for the prime minister's office complex depicts a golden sheaf of curved wheat, set high on a pedestal in a long, sloping landscape. Initial design concepts for the sculpture were quite different, however. A huge statue of King Hussein was proposed. The king would not allow it. Baghdad's Victory Arch, built in 1989, provides a considerable contrast. It consists of two huge forearms grasping swords that cross at the center of the arch. The arms actually represent enlarged casts of Saddam Hussein's arms, showing every bump and follicle; they epitomize the excesses of the expression of cultural identity and national heritage that Samir Al-Khalil says is so rampant in the Arab world (1991).

In pre-1977 Baghdad there were three major public sculptures, one of General Maude, a British commander; one of King Faisal; and the third was of Prime Minister As-Sa'doun. The first two were destroyed in 1958; the third was kept to remind the populace of colonialism. Iraq under Saddam attempted to establish continuity with previous civilizations through its museums and public art projects, much as Egypt did. However, Al-Khalil, citing Saddam's government's preoccupation with inventing its cultural identity, has argued that there was in fact no continuity with the historic past (1991, 69–70).

How have Jordan's contemporary art museums—at the Darat al Funun and in the Jordan National Gallery—handled such issues of identity and continuity? And how, if at all, are these institutions of modern art used by the government to develop cultural identity? Could these institutions be used to manipulate history for social control? Is the art hanging on the walls directly related to the maintenance of the monarchy, the perpetuation of ideal Bedouin virtues? Is Palestinian art restricted? Do these institutions promote religious tenets or grand descent from ancient cultures? Are their walls covered with overtly patriotic or patently moralistic or nationalistic themes, or does one find diversity, free artistic expression, and perhaps even a nude represented?

Since my first visit to the National Gallery in 1982, and over the years since, I have never observed an exhibition of blatant nationalistic propaganda or one featuring portraits of the king; nor have the exhibits exclusively promoted the monarchy. The works on view have been divided between abstraction and realism with figurative painting, sculpture, and calligraphy represented. Painting has always seemed to dominate the exhibitions—over sculpture, graphics, and photography. Both the number of works on view and the quality have increased. Personal and social themes in the art works shared wall space with expressions of pop culture, reflections of Qur'anic calligraphy, empathy with the Intifada, expressionist feminist outrage, realistic seductive allure, and architectural design. Although the works were not even on the flap of the envelope to challenge, mock, or degrade Islamic society, where was the portrait of the king? One could be found on the wall of founder Wijdan Ali's office. The image of King Hussein was also found in Amman at an exhibition of children's art at the Haya Cultural Center in March of 1999, where his portrait was featured in celebration of his return from medical treatment in the United States. As is common in monarchies, the king's image dominated the Stamp Museum and the Central Bank's Numismatic Museum, and his photograph often appears in businesses and shops.

The Darat al Funun holds annual exhibits of its stable of contemporary local artists and features Arab artists from throughout the world. The works vary in media and message. Because the sales component is important in the development of these exhibitions, the market logically plays a part in determining content, but the financial independence of the institution, its founding policies, its international ties, and its commitment to arts education through its library, Internet services, lectures, symposia, and films keep it an open and apolitical forum. Founder Suha Shoman made it clear in conversations that she would not promote exhibitions that were based solely on politics.

To what do we attribute these policies and this open freedom of expression? First, these institutions were inspired by women who had broad understanding of existing museum models and who from the outset established nongovernmental, nonprofit institutions with forward thinking, experienced personnel and committees that participated in operation and governance. Second, the funding for both of these institutions is predominantly from private individuals, other cultural nonprofits, foundations, and businesses. Third, both internationally educated founders are artists, and one is Palestinian. With this kind of background, these institutions were not likely to exclude presentations vis-à-vis the Jordanian/Palestinian issue or limit artistic expression.

Attitudes, Goals, and the Woman's Touch

In the United States, John Cotton Dana proclaimed: "In almost every community, large or small today, it will be easier to find a woman than a man who is fitted to the director's task and is willing to take it" (1917, 27). Is this universal?

What seems to make museum work an acceptable, even desirable, profession for women? Could it be the exclusivity, or the perceived idea that collecting, displaying, and inventorying is women's work? Are there few other opportunities for women professionals? Is it the controlled environment—is it an allowed profession? Could it be there is status in working for the government—or is it because of the government's health care provisions and retirement plan? Or, is museum work the only non-physical option for those with a degree in archeology? Is it acceptable because it is a motherly profession in a patriarchal society? Could the choice be a passion for order, or a statement of pride in one's heritage? Luck? Chance? These and other issues converge in the search to better understand the dynamics of women and museums in the Kingdom of Jordan.

Tucker points out the major influence women have had on the development of cultural life in the Middle East, especially in the realm of high culture that includes written poetry, novels, and song (1988, 88). This is true in the visual arts and the museum profession as well. Further, she cites the upper-class tradition of educating women that produced several "women of letters" in the nineteenth century. That tradition laid the foundation for women to play a central role in the development of new art forms in the twentieth century, including the visual arts.

How dedicated these women were is sometimes questioned, however. Critiquing their involvement, Wijdan Ali commented: "Fine arts seemed to attract women who became interested in arts as a hobby rather than a career" (1999). As a tangent observation, many of the museum founders and cultural leaders in Jordan were artists themselves. Of the eight women artists who live and work in Jordan who were featured in the "Forces of Change: Artists of the Arab World" exhibition organized by the International Council for Women in the Arts and the National Museum of Women in the Arts in 1994, all are represented in the collection of the Jordan National Gallery, and five have been involved in museum development.

Why is there such a high percentage of women working in Jordan's museums? My research has indicated that museum work is among the career options available for university archeology and anthropology graduates, but is availability the reason it is chosen? Love of history and a desire to be near the artifacts of history are perhaps logical and universal reasons for choosing a career devoted to the investigation and presentation of objects, as is a love for one's heritage and a passion for descriptive order and research.

Studies have shown that there appears to be a very low preference among females in Muslim countries for becoming sales workers, an occupation in which the likelihood of indiscriminate contact with outsiders is high (Mujahid 1985, 114). This fact might reinforce the thought that women who work in museums are in some way protected from public contact or that there is an aura of isolation or exclusivity about the work. Perceptions such as "Only nice people come to museums, so it's a career women are safe in" (Tukan 1998) reflect the idea that there is an association of respectability about museums and that is why women are attracted to them. Not only are there fewer men in that arena, it follows that those who are there are also more respectable.

None of the women interviewed attributed their choice of career to chance. Each woman had a story, a reason, and the determination to get where she now was. That is not to say they all were satisfied, or were not sometimes disillusioned with the work they were doing or the situation they were in. Their work situations, often frustrating and static, were seldom attributed to the fact that they were female, for there were men who worked in lesser positions than they did, as guards and maintenance and support help. Women and men shared the benefits and physical disadvantages of their museums together. On a cold day in January, I found both men and women employees huddled around a portable stove in the center of the small room behind the admissions desk at Amman's Archeological Museum. Everyone was cold; equal opportunity discomfort.

Several women were discouraged from a career in archeology or museology. Nazmieh Rida Tawfiq Darwish confided that her professor at the university asked her why she wanted to go into archeology, telling her: "That's a goat's life." She rebutted, "I want to be a goat" (Darwish 1999).

Some women seemed destined to work in museums. Kilani became dedicated when she met Sa'adieh Al Tel, director of the Museum of Popular Traditions; Wijdan Ali when she saw the need for a place to showcase Jordan's fine arts; likewise, Suha Shoman when she saw the need for a place where artists, writers, and musicians could freely interact and explore creativity and knew she could develop such a place.

Masaadeh seemed destined for her work in a museum. She followed in the footsteps of her parents. Although they had no professional training for their work in Kerak's museums, they were an early support system for her and helped her define her goals. She faced many obstacles in her pursuit of a career in archeology. Coming from a small town, she was told: "Here in Jordan they say archeology isn't for girls" (Masaadeh 1999). While conducting fieldwork for her degree, she went to work at five in the morning and came back home dirty and covered with dust. Initially townspeople criticized her and told her that her work was for a man. "But the next year they stopped me in the street and asked me what I did. Now, they're used to me, but always they ask if I found the gold yet" (Masaadeh 1999).

For Huda Kilani, museum work was also an early goal. She recalled visiting the Museum of Popular Traditions in downtown Amman while still a student at the university and speaking with Muna Zaglow about the museum's collections and activities. She was told they needed help. That was all it took. Learning from Al Tel about the textiles, weavings, jewelry, and costumes in the collection fascinated her, and she soon became committed to museum work. "I've reached my goal. . . . To be a curator was my dream. And you don't get your goals easily" (Kilani 1999b).

Interest in Jordan's history and in the material culture of the past was the reason Eman al-Qudah, Kilani's classmate in archeology and curator of the Folklore Museum, chose museum work. She sought a career in museums because "I'm interested in the traditional life in Jordan" (al-Qudah 1999b), and working in a museum allowed her to be near the objects. Eman Oweis has worked many years in her chosen field in Jerash. Museum work has allowed her to combine her many areas of interest: "Initially I wanted to study philosophy, later history. I like history, I wanted to know more about the past" (Oweis 1999b).

Other women, including Lubna Hashem, were inspired by the abundant antiquities around them. Hashem credited her family for instilling a love of museums in her, and recalled how she accompanied them when they traveled abroad and visited museums (Hashem 1999). Siham Balqar drew upon her experience of living in a land rich in antiquities to choose her career. For her, working in a museum seemed to have many assets: "dealing with the objects, the visitors . . . and the research" (Balqar 1999). Seated beside Balqar in her museum office during an interview, curator Tamara Bermamet added her voice on the advantages of working in museums: "It's near the things I love. It's the best place to be, when you study archeology . . . in the museum" (Bermamet 1999). And, in apparent reference to other colleagues choosing fieldwork: "We have a roof over our head. It's nicer here, there's no mud."

There are several ways to approach museum work. One is to work within a system, another is to create a new entity. The difference is not just opportunity, education, or economic class, but vision. Some museum founders, including Sa'adieh Al Tel, Hidea Abaza, Nazmieh Rida Tawfiq Darwish, and Aida Naghawi, created regional museums for the Department of Antiquities and Awqaf. But the challenge of founding a museum, of creating a private institution where none yet existed—and making it work—attracted both Wijdan Ali and Suha Shoman. They had vision. Regardless of their approach to the profession, all these women sought to be respected administrators, sometimes in an uncooperative and culturally inattentive environment.

During a tour of the new museum in Irbid, Ruba Abu Dalu radiated enthusiasm for her work. She negotiated the muddy construction, involved the architects in discussion, provided detailed information on the structure, programming, educational outreach, and philosophy of the new museum, and, she added: "I chose to work in this museum because it will recount the story of mankind . . . and preserve this heritage" (Abu Dalu 1998b).

Most of the women interviewed believed that women had special or unique aptitudes that they could bring to museum work. As a woman, most felt they were better suited for the job of curator than a man. In Aqaba, Al Fakhri noted that women "have a *touch*. We save things in the home and we know how to decorate—from our mothers. And as a mother myself, I can talk to children. Women have a special touch" (1999). Also recognizing women's unique aptitudes was Kilani: "Museums need a woman's touch, and women are more suitable for this work." But then she added, "Men are better at administration" (1999a). Oweis concurred: "Women have a way . . . to show the objects, to show them well. I make the displays, we women sew. And for the tourists, women can speak well . . . and be friendly" (1999a). Masaadeh continued in that vein, mentioning that she added a feminine touch to her museum environment. "I brought plants into the office, helped to redecorate when I came, and I clean often. Men don't notice these things" (1999).

Were the speakers of these comments implying that curatorial work in museums was not a man's job and that museum administration was a man's job? These women seem to see no stereotyping of the sexes; they concentrate on their professional success.

From a man's perspective, Nayef Goussous, director and curator of the new Numismatic Museum of the Jordan National Bank, observed that there were "many women in numismatics. They have more patience. Additionally, women in the workplace are men and ladies at the same time, because of their obligations in the home and the workplace" (Goussous 1999).

Although a majority of curatorial and administrative positions in government-sponsored and university museums were held by men, thirteen of the twenty-nine positions were held by women. In discussion and on questionnaires, all curators in my research group denied government policies of preference for men in the workforce. They cited the equal pay scale for men and women and mentioned the fact that any preference "is not necessary now . . . or, maybe it was before, with older men" (Hadidi 1999). Concerning preferences for male workers, Oweis felt it was "the contrary. Women hold higher positions in most museums in Jordan" (1999a), and Abu Dalu thought "the opposite was right. That they prefer women in museum jobs more than men" (1998a).

Other women acknowledged that men might have been given the advantage for jobs right after the draft ended when the peace treaty with Israel was signed. One retired female administrator concluded: "In general, men in Jordan have the advantage of employment—but not in museums. However, it would never happen that a lady becomes director general of the department" (Balqar 1999). A former curator who had just returned from Canada with a master's degree in museology suggested that preferences exist "maybe at the upper management levels" (Al-Kurdi 1999).

Given these attitudes about preferences, did the women in this study believe they had the same goals or opportunities as their male coworkers? Among the older women in government museums, several said yes (in the museums in Salt, Jerash, and Amman); others said "not yet" (Hadidi 1999).

Two curators felt that although the incentives to work were the same, such as equal pay, they were not interested in adding more administrative responsibilities to their jobs: "I don't want to be the director. There's too much responsibility. I have enough at home" (Bermamet 1998), and "It is not part of my personality to be on top" (Kilani 1999a). But quite the opposite view came from two women from the private museum sector who asserted themselves: "I am competitive, my goal is to be assistant director or director" (Al-Kurdi 1999), and another declared her "ambition was to go solo" (Mufti 1999).

Many women, including Bermamet and Oweis, expressed their personal goals through reference to the goals of their institution. Bermamet's goal was "to help visitors, especially children, understand the history of Jordan" (1998), and Oweis wanted to help plan a "garden inside the ruins of Jerash . . . and a hotel and a whole new museum for mosaics, marble statues, and inscriptions" (1999a).

In the broader context, two administrators who set their own goals spoke of the future: Wijdan Ali's objective is "the promotion of world peace through the advancement of the arts and the eradication of cultural apartheid" (1998), and Suha Shoman references President John F. Kennedy's concept of service: "We should be doing something for the country. We are, as artists, witnesses of our time; we are the true historians. We should be doing something for the country" (Shoman 1999).

With their passion and dedication, would these women advocate museum work to their daughters? Several women said their daughters were interested in museum careers and they encouraged this interest. Ali's daughter Rajwa is an artist who has participated curatorially at the Darat al Funun, and mention has already been made of Zayyaden's daughter following in her footsteps at Kerak.

What advice would these curators and administrators give to women just entering the museum profession? Some gave practical advice, others shared personal thoughts: "Read a lot. Work from the heart," advised Eman Oweis (1999b); "Have a lot of patience and a good command of foreign languages," and, "If they work in a government-sponsored museum, they should know that not all the things they wish would come true" (Bermamet 1999).

"They should believe in what they are doing," said Kilani (1999b); Hadidi advocates "specific study to include this field; [to be] more social than any other women; [to have] good experience, to participate in educational events, lectures at institutions, schools, universities and to follow the local mayor and his activities" (1999).

Abu Dalu challenged newcomers: "Love this work as a thing private and special; try to know and learn as much as possible about museum work, then everything will come" (1998a). Lastly, Shoman's advice to others is: "We need to pass things on to the next generation. Fahrelnissa gave me a vision. I want to pass it on" (1999).

A common satisfaction for museum workers is their proximity to objects of beauty or importance. Given the daily interaction with exhibits and collections, it is not surprising that museum workers would be collectors themselves. Sa'adieh Al Tel's home in Amman (both she and Samia Zaru designed their own homes) "had many things. . . . Her house was like a museum" (Kilani 1999a). Also interested in the traditional and the ancient, Sawsan Al-Fakhri collects reproductions of Nabataean pottery (1999). Zaru's home and grounds are filled with paintings and sculpture, many her own, much of it reflecting Palestinian iconography. Ali's collecting reflects her love of contemporary art, calligraphy, and books (1999). Several other women also mentioned their love of books. Naghawi (1999) collects books on archeology, and Al-Kurdi collects children's books. Tied to her interest in interior design, Mufti (1999) collects miniature objects such as furniture for dollhouses. Oweis (1999a) uses her artistic skills to make puppets—and puts on puppet shows for children. Shoman collects art works, "but not for investment—for support" (1999). Perhaps the strongest response to my inquiries about personal collecting came from Al-Kurdi, who commented on the issue as it involved antiquities. She voiced her opposition to personal ownership of what is state property and should be governed by professional ethics. "It's against the law. Some department people got in trouble in the past" (Al-Kurdi 1999). She also felt strongly about professionalism, arguing: "There is no code of ethics. One is needed." Her convictions led her to express an interest in starting a professional museum association in Jordan (Al-Kurdi 1999).

Twelve Case Studies

The Museum as Educator:
Archeology Museum, University of Jordan

A museum is an education center—not a warehouse.

—Wijdan Ali

Established in 1962, the same year the University of Jordan was founded, the Archaeology Museum is also referred to as the Archeological Museum in official literature.

Located in a central area on the campus, where streets and walkways meet, the landscaped entrance enclave, lined with marble statuary, funereal memorials, and architectural remnants, is hard to miss. Much of the material in the collection is from excavations conducted by the archeology department of the university itself. The museum participates in the teaching program where students participate in actual fieldwork as well as receive historical, classification, conservation, and restoration experience on artifacts. The museum is an academic center dedicated to research in archeology and offers its facilities to the teaching staff of the Department of Archeology. The museum states that its goals are to:

- Intensify knowledge of Jordan's heritage;
- Organize traveling exhibits;
- Develop the museum in accordance with the scientific status of the university;
- Establish cooperation with national and international scientific departments and institutions;

47

· Document the collections properly;
· Keep comprehensive records; and
· Teach applied courses in archeology. (Department of Antiquities 1994, 6)

Director of the museum for the past five years is Manal Awamleh, a graduate of the archeology degree program at the university. She takes pride in her responsibilities and the educational role she plays in "giving tours, meeting people and scholars from different places. It's the best part of my job" (Awamleh 1999). Only schoolchildren from the higher grades visit the museum; younger ones visit the adjoining National Heritage Museum of which she is also the administrator.

What are her goals for the Archeological Museum? "To build a new one with better technology and a better laboratory where we will treat objects from the excavations." And her goals for herself? She would like a master's degree in archeology, however, she cites the difficulties: "I have children, my work, and my home" (Awamleh 1999).

The National Heritage Museum at the University of Jordan, also known as the Anthropological Museum of the University of Jordan, adjoins the Archeological Museum on the campus and has a different history, purpose, and exhibit philosophy. In 1977 the university's Department of Sociology responded to the need for a collection that reflected the traditional lifestyle of Jordanian society in the villages and the Badia (eastern desert region) to complement its theoretical coursework. The collections developed from several sources. Initially under the supervision of Professor A. Rabay'ah from the sociology department, the collections expanded through purchases and gifts from the community. Many students also donated objects representative of their Jordanian heritage. Finally, in 1980 the museum was established.

The exhibit hall contains vignettes displaying the utilitarian objects used in food gathering and production, clothing adornment and manufacture, and ceremonial and hospitality events, as well as cases and displays of weapons, tools, and folk medicine.

As with other ethnographic museums in Jordan, this museum displays objects made by and for women and reflects the traditional Jordanian social structure. Thus the majority of the items and the exhibits represent women and involve either female mannequins engaged in domestic chores or the products of women's work such as costume, straw work, and weaving. The display of the woman's section of a Bedouin tent (*beit al-sha'ir*) includes both personal and utilitarian items in a realistic setting that the visitor can walk into.

Continuity and Dialogue in the House of Arts: The Darat al Funun

> Suha Shoman is a demanding patron, [and] strains to build the gallery on high artistic standards.
>
> *—Wijdan Ali*

The concept of the Darat al Funun reaches far beyond mere display of art works. It encompasses teaching, workshops, a reference and video library, Internet services, a lecture series, films, gallery talks, publications—and, given its extensive grounds, performing arts programs of theater, dance, and music. It has become an art center in the full sense of the word, one with international participation and influence. The Dara also has on permanent display a small exhibition of artifacts found on its premises during restoration and construction of the site. Although its programming and name reflect that of an art center, it acts also as a museum.

The nonprofit parent organization, the Abdul Hameed Shoman Foundation, was established by the Arab Bank in 1978 to promote knowledge and research and to develop the sciences, humanities, and the arts. Although the foundation initiated a gallery in 1988 at a site in the Shmeisani area of Amman that was called the Cultural and Scientific Center of the Shoman Foundation, the creation of the Darat al Funun at its present site on Jebel Weibde was the vision of Suha Shoman, wife of the chairman of the Arab Bank. She is credited as the founder. Two other women assisted in this development, Rajwa bint Ali and Muna Deeb. In developing the concept and choosing the site, Shoman admitted she was a product of the 1968 artists' revolt in Paris. She was there. She heard the artists claim that museums were for dead people: "But the Dara is proving our culture is very much alive—with continuity and the product of our past" (Shoman 1999). In choosing the site for the Dara, she referred to an incident when she made a professional evaluation of the first modern prison in Lebanon: "It was a beautiful building, but there was no consideration given to the human part—the inside was empty. You need doctors, psychologists, criminologists, sociologists. . . . You need people to work together. . . . The analogy to the Dara is that we need an infrastructure, not just a building" (Shoman 1999). Her vision of a place to showcase the arts, encourage artists, and serve as an educational resource for the community became a reality in 1993. Her convictions were strong and her task formidable: "If the Shoman Foundation gets involved with art, it has to do so with the same standards as we do other projects. I took over the art part. There was not any information on how you present a show . . . how you light it . . . the ABCs of how you prepare an exhibit!" (Shoman 1999).

Initially, for guidance, an international board composed of artists and scholars met annually with Shoman to discuss the nuts and bolts, the development of programs, and the long-range plans. Members of the board were Khalid Shoman, Suha Shoman, Ibrahim Alaway, Mai Mathafa, Farouk Jaber, Kamal Boullata, and Samia Halaby. These meetings later became individual consultations (Maher 1998).

But the Dara might never have become a reality—even with the available funding—if not for the influence of Fahrelnissa Zeid. Arriving in Amman in the mid-1970s, this internationally known artist with ties to the Hashemite dynasty opened the Fahrelnissa Zeid Royal Institute of Fine Arts in her home. Shoman became one of her students. There, she learned more than the history of art and personal artistic creativity, and she made a commitment to carry on the legacy of her mentor. Shoman spares no opportunity to credit the philosophy and teaching of Fahrelnissa Zeid for the development of the Dara (1999).

While functioning in the present and preparing for the future, the ancient history of the Dara complex is noteworthy. The site incorporates the remains of a sixth-century Byzantine church built over a Roman temple. Three of the four caves on the property show remains of mosaic floors. In 1993, the Shoman Foundation, in cooperation with the Jordanian Department of Antiquities, began excavations at the site under the direction of Pierre Bikai of the American Center of Oriental Research.

In 1918, the governor of Salt, Nimer Pasha al-Hmoud, built the main house above the church. It is there that Peake Pasha, the former British commander of the Arab Legion, lived from 1921 to 1938. The building housed the British Officers Club from 1938 to 1956, and until 1975 the Arab School for Girls. The two upper houses, one used today as gallery space and offices, the other a guest house, were constructed during the 1920s; the guest house was the home of Emir Abdullah's court poet.

Uninhabited when the foundation began looking for a site that was close to public services and the downtown area, the lower building fulfilled a double purpose: preserving the country's architectural heritage and bringing art to a populated part of the city. Renovation by Ammar Khammash honored the indigenous architecture of early Amman, and the newly built areas reflected the influence of early Islamic designs and the architecture of the desert castles. Great attention was paid to integrating these three houses and ancient ruins into a functional and aesthetic campus. This was accomplished through terraced, landscaped walkways, integrated design, and lighting. The three galleries in the main building have been adapted to present and protect works of art. The long narrow rooms retain their original decorated floor tiles and converge at a semicircular glassed patio that confronts the Old City of Amman in the distance.

The extensive reference library, vaulted in a design reminiscent of the Umayyad desert castle Qasr el Amra, was built atop the roof of the main building. It contains publications on art, art criticism, and art techniques from the Islamic world, Europe, Asia, Africa, and the Americas. Ancient as well as contemporary art is represented, and there are small sections on feminist art and international museums. A computer database on Arab art and artists can be accessed, and the library maintains a Web site on the Internet with pages for its stable of seventy artists. Other educational opportunities include lectures by visiting artists and historians and the weekly "Thursday Art Meetings" where film or videos and discussions often center on the world's major art movements. Many of these programs, films, and videos are in English.

There are three reasons that the Darat al Funun operates so professionally: funding, staff, and leadership. Guaranteed a percentage of profit from the Arab Bank annually, the Dara's programs, record keeping, maintenance, staff salaries, utilities—and all other aspects of its operation—are maintained, and new initiatives can be developed as well. The staff members are qualified, professional, and dedicated. They exude an attitude of helpfulness and competence, and are multilingual.

The goals of the Dara are broad: to make the library an information and resource center of Jordanian, Arab, and international art; to display regular exhibitions of Jordanian and Arab artists; to provide open studios in printmaking and sculpture; and to promote art appreciation among the Jordanian public, especially by reaching out to schoolchildren, teachers, and other groups. The multidisciplined summer festivals with their wide range of visual, performing arts, and teaching activities are also concerned with connoisseurship. They support the concept of the arts as "measurable," by featuring work by students in the programs.

Another purpose of the institution is the promotion and sale of works exhibited by its stable of artists. Artists are selected by submission of slides and résumés to the director. The board and staff make the decisions. There is no commission on sales. Although there is no "official" permanent collection from this body of work, a selection is kept in storage on the premises, and many pieces are on display in the offices. Herein lies one of the few criticisms heard about the Dara and its policies. Not only does the program reflect many of the same artists year after year, but also local artists feel their work is not promoted as well as it could be. This might be accomplished better if a staff position was created for the purpose of sales; given the programming at the Dara, it is not possible for staff to focus solely on this aspect of their operation.

In an article for the *Jordan Times* on the tenth anniversary exhibition of the Dara, I credited the institution as providing a unique experience in Jordan—one obviously honed from judicious study of major art centers worldwide (Malt 1999). I noted that the Darat al Funun added its own meaning and focus to the models of other art centers, creating an educational, historical, archeological, and aesthetic entity with the potential to develop and promote cultural heritage through contemporary artistic expression.

The issues of judicious study and wise application of policy from museums in the West drew comments from the founder—just as it did from the founder of the Jordan National Gallery. Shoman stressed that what was suitable for the development and operation of the Dara was not a literal transfer of American or European policies, but a working policy based on the present needs, capabilities, and uniqueness of Jordan (1999). Although the Dara is committed to and maintains high professional standards in museology, both the director and the founder discussed the policies (especially for borrowing) of American museums as restrictive and encumbering.

An example of the Dara's activities for the period August 24 through September 30, 1999, follows:

Exhibitions

> Fifty Years of Graphic Art from Iraq
> Alia Ammoura: "A Spirit of Beauty"
> Computer art by the Jordanian group Passe
> Opening ceremony for the Summer Academy of Art: Marwan Qassab Bashi

Lectures and Events

> Iraqi artist Rafa' Nasiri: "Fifty Years of Iraqi Graphic Art"
> Jordanian writer Elias Farkouh: readings of his short stories
> Book signing, writer Abdel-Rahman Muneef: *Ard Al Sawad*
> Syrian artist Marwan: "Between Profession and Creativity"
> Iraqi musician Asad Mohammad Ali: "Arab Music"
> Jordanian artist Abdul Raouf Ahamoum: "Alia Ammoura, a Spirit of Beauty"

Music Performances

> Concert by the Jordanian group Ethereal
> Classical music by the Iraqi group Somer

Thursday Art Meeting (Videos and Films in English)

> Lectures and films on graphic art since the sixteenth century

No Faux—Forever Folk: The Folklore Museum

Our greatest need is to develop technology.
—Eman al-Qudah

In 1973, charged by the successful activity of the Museum of Popular Traditions in the eastern side of the Roman Theater in downtown Amman, Hidea Abaza began planning and collecting for a sister museum in the western section. This new folklore museum was to focus on Jordan's recent cultural heritage through the exhibition of objects from the three distinct geographical and societal groups in Jordan, the Bedouin of the desert, the villager, and the city dweller. Vignettes were planned and installed to portray all aspects of daily life and domestic activities in the five exhibit halls. Today, these exhibits have not seen much change; there is little explanatory labeling in the cases or rooms, and lighting can vary with the weather conditions. The collections, however, represent fine period examples.

Abaza, credited as the founder, took over the responsibilities of director and began collecting material for the displays. She drew on her work experience with Sa'adieh Al Tel in the Museum of Popular Traditions, and eventually there developed a competitive atmosphere between the two women—prompting one museum to be called "Sa'adieh's place" and the other "Hidea's place." Both were strong women. Unlike Al Tel, Abaza was an employee of the Department of Antiquities and spent a great deal of her time searching the countryside for suitable items for the collection. Trained as a lawyer, she was an effective museum spokesperson and was credited by Antiquities director Ghazi Bisheh as "initiating regional museums" (Bisheh 1999).

When Abaza retired, Eman al-Qudah (Iyman El Qudah) was appointed curator, and the director general of the Department of Antiquities was appointed to the directorship of the museum. Al-Qudah received her bachelor's degree in archeology from the University of Jordan. She began work in the museum because she was interested in traditional life in Jordan, and she confided that her goal was to "help develop the museum I work in to become one of the famous museums in the region" (al-Qudah 1999b). Her museology training, like that of many of the young curators in government museums, consisted of a semester in museum exhibit design at the University of Jordan, a core curriculum course of the archeology degree program. She saw her biggest challenge as proving herself in the field of folklore (al-Qudah 1999b).

In an article for ICOM, al-Qudah outlined the problems facing the museum, many of them relating to its location in a historic monument, the very asset that draws much of its audience. Among the problems discussed are inadequate space for exhibiting the objects of Jordan's cultural heritage properly, the lack of a library and storage areas, the disintegration of the limestone structure itself, and pollution from the urban setting (al-Qudah 1994).

Jordan's Gem: The Geological Museum

The Geology Museum, it's fabulous: mahogany paneling, with rocks, sharks teeth, but no one goes!

—*Hind Nasser*

The Geological Museum of the National Resources Authority displays the very physical structure of Jordan. Devoted to presentation of earth sciences, the museum exhibits Jordan's rocks, fossils, minerals, and natural resources in the context of their physical environment, historical epoch, and economic usage. The multimedia displays begin with general information on geology, the formation of the earth and planets, and their evolution, then become specific to Jordan and its industry, current exploration, and mining. Labels and informative wall text are in both Arabic and English.

The large wooden cases in the halls contain examples of the physical structure of the different areas of Jordan. These displays and the sample teaching kits the museum provides to educational institutions are upgraded continually as specimens are brought in by Survey Division personnel who spend at least seven days a month out in the field.

Curator Suhair Shadid, directorate administrator for the museum, holds a degree in geology from the University of Jordan, as does her assistant, Asma Zu'bi. For Shadid, the purpose of the museum is basic: "To tell visitors about the geology of Jordan and geology in general" (1999). This is a working museum, and it is evident as she actively seeks publications on the natural sciences. Students of all ages, from the public schools to the universities, visit as a practical part of their curriculum. Her responsibilities include specimen labeling, text information for the dioramas and publications, collections management, preparation of loan exhibits, and giving guided tours.

When visited in April of 1999, Shadid was preparing an exhibit to be called "The Evolution of Life." "I will do it simply, for all ages to understand. It is a big responsibility," she explained (1999). Knowing the project's importance, her first step was research on similar projects internationally, looking for ideas on the presentation and interpretation. In response to a question about the philosophy behind the presentation, whether it would be Darwinian or creationist, she answered it would be evolutionist.

The Old Is New: Irbid Archeological Museum

Museums have stories, from prehistory to today; they can talk.

—*Ruba Abu Dalu*

Winding through the large, busy city of Irbid, passing sidewalk cafes on wide streets, with green and red tulip lights planted in the median, then turning inward through the downtown's narrow souk on the way to the museum, one notices that most of the women on the street wear Western clothing and almost all are scarved. This contrasts with the public appearance of women in the streets of Amman.

At the Ottoman prison that is being restored and readapted into a museum, the architects explain their dilemma. What should they keep or restore: the oldest walls and tiles? The most beautiful ones? The rarest ones? The prison complex, dating from the nineteenth century, has had several uses and reflects many external and interior architectural adaptations. The architects solved their restoration problems by leaving examples from all periods. For instance, they kept the 1940s Syrian tile work in the upstairs rooms, they uncovered and kept the original niches in the walls, and they removed plaster to expose the stonework wherever possible.

The new multipurpose building will serve several audiences when it is finished: tourist and student visitors to the museum; conservationists (a small room presently is being used for mosaic restoration); administrators, educators, and staff of the Department of Antiquities, whose offices will be on the second floor; researchers, who will have access to archives and a library; and concertgoers, who can experience performing arts programs in the large walled courtyard.

Curator of the old Irbid Museum at the Department of Antiquities building, assistant inspector of archeology, and preparing to be the future director of this new museum complex is Ruba Abu Dalu. A native of Irbid, her bachelor's degree was in fine arts with a specialty in Islamic architecture and interior design, and her master's thesis, in Islamic archeology, was on the sugar mills of the Jordan Valley. She explained that education was always important in her family. Her sisters have graduate degrees, and her mother has been active in women's organizations (Abu Dalu 1998a).

Her plans for the new museum are comprehensive: "The museum should serve as a major center for documenting and preserving the cultural heritage of Jordan and its natural and human history; for conservation and restoration of all materials related to cultural and natural history; for programs and services to the public; for special educational programs for schools, and it should be seen as an academic institution for the study of collections and related aspects as well as for the development of museology. It should be a dynamic center" (Abu Dalu 1998b).

Abu Dalu's major focus will be creating an educational center, not just a display hall or storage place for collections, and she envisions in-house and outreach educational programs for schoolchildren as well as practical training for students in the fields of museology and conservation. She plans to equip the new facility with computers for inventory and data control, and for research and communication between scholars.

Still Grand after All These Years:
Jerash Archeological Museum

Jordan is an open museum.
—*Hasan Ayed 1996*

Gerasa, ancient Jerash, representative of diverse cultures and religions and rich in the beauty of its architecture, mosaics, statuary, and arts lay in ruins until 1806. In 1920, the Department of Antiquities began reconstruction of several sites. In 1923 or 1925, depending on the source (*Jordan Times* 2000), the vault underneath the Temple of Artemis was prepared for the display of many of the important archeological objects found on the site. Gradually a major collection was amassed, drawing worldwide attention to the facility—but that facility was unable to hold or present the artifacts properly. Development of the site proceeded under the British director of Antiquities, G. Lankester Harding, between 1936 and 1956. So many objects (more than half a million) have been collected that even today, with a new museum facility, storage is a problem.

Jerash was identified early on as an important historical resource for the newly independent country because it is one of the best-preserved ancient Roman sites in the world. It was one of the cities of the Decapolis. The Roman emperor Hadrian wintered in Jerash in 129–30 c.e. and built a triumphal arch most of which stands today. The city itself, founded after the time of Alexander the Great, reflected its wealth by ostentatious building programs—two Roman baths, three theaters, fountains, shops, temples—all possible because of the abundant water supply. The physical and cultural amenities at that time earned Jerash the name "the city of lazy generals" (Fistere and Fistere n.d., n.p.).

Political, religious, and social changes transformed Jerash. Christians arrived during the fourth century and converted many pagan temples to churches; in 635, Muslim armies conquered the city; earthquakes in the eighth and ninth centuries were instrumental in its decline as a regional trading center.

In 1985, archeologist Aida Naghawi, a graduate of the University of Jordan, became the first curator of the museum. In an article on Jerash, Wijdan Ali commented on the contemporary importance of this ancient city and the size of its new museum: "A small museum at each important archeological site in Jordan is a refreshing idea and the Jerash museum is the first. People can identify more easily with a small museum than with a huge imposing one that more often overwhelms the visitor than impresses him" (Ali 1996, 9).

The new museum at the site is located in a restored building that had been built first to accommodate Department of Antiquities employees in the 1930s, then became a tourist rest house in 1962. It features the exhibit "Jordan in History" (Oweis 1994, 173). Today, this facility has become too small.

Eman Oweis, the present curator for the Department of Antiquities, has worked in Jerash on excavations and archeological planning for more than eighteen years; twelve of those years have been at the museum as a curator and conservator. A graduate in history and archeology from the University of Damascus, she has additional training in conservation from Yarmouk University. Her talents are also evident in exhibit design, as she often uses her sewing skills to make displays. The large low semicircular riser near the office that displays stone artifacts on its stitched fabric covering is an example of her work. The riser formerly hung upside down from the ceiling as an interior space divider.

For many years she has made puppets, creating shows for children around Christmas and Easter themes. She envisions expanding that hobby to create a puppet show that would explain the history of Jerash to children—either presenting it on site or taking it to the schools.

A small side room partitioned from her office is lined with shelves holding artifacts brought to her for restoration, registration, study, or classification. Many of the boxes on the shelves also contain ceramic shards or broken glass vials that have been confiscated from poachers by the local police. "If we had found them," she said, "we'd have all the pieces. Guards keep poachers from digging inside the site, but not outside. Visitors and townspeople are sometimes caught with objects they have found in the huge site, and enforcement is a major problem. Locally, police go to the homes and either confiscate the pieces or register and photograph them, allowing them to be kept" (Oweis 1999a). The sheer amount of archeological material available makes theft an ongoing problem.

Also in the side room is a small table on which she identifies and cleans coins. Oweis feels being a woman has distinct advantages in her job. "Women have a way with exhibit design. I clean the coins and read them . . . very detailed . . . and we can speak well to visitors." She cares for and about the museum and considers it her life: "My life is in the past and in the future" (Oweis 1999a).

In her 1994 article for ICOM, Oweis outlines modern methods for museum construction, as well as for storage, presentation, and cost-effective conservation of collections. She offers suggestions for the improvement of the Jerash museum and the museum experience at the site and speaks of the possibility of a new museum for the mosaics and marble statuary—perhaps in the Zeus temple area. She also recommends a major hotel be built in the area so that tourists can stay near the site, and the creation of a garden space for visitors within the site.

Museum Sclerosis: The Jordan Archeological Museum

The Citadel museum was the right size for the 1950s, now it's too small.
—*Tamara Bermamet*

The heady confrontation with exquisite examples of the past is tempered by bone-chilling cold in winter and the sheer number of the objects presented. The small, cramped "temple to antiquity" was built in 1951–52 on the Citadel hill (Jabal al-Qala'a), overlooking Amman amid dramatic Roman ruins. It is one of the few museums in Jordan that was actually built to be a museum. "Even the metal showcases were custom made to fit the space" (Balqar and Zayyat 1994, 156).

True to tradition, the design of the Jordan Archeological Museum represented the prevailing international museum-temple taste of the decade. It contains objects spanning the Paleolithic to the Mamluk periods. Although other museums in Jordan usually focus on objects from their immediate area, this museum contains artifacts from all the archeological sites in the country. The sheer number of items on display is overwhelming and somewhat distracting, perhaps detrimental to the true value and individual respect the objects deserve, as many objects are barely inches apart in their cases. Cabinets and cases jumbled together divide the small facility, while the walls loom with statuary. Perhaps the sheer size of the collections is daunting not only to the visitor but also to the keepers, whose responsibility they are, as displays seldom change and new information is seldom added. Although acknowledging the importance of this museum and the others in Jordan, author/commentator/publisher Rami Khouri concludes: "The potential is enormous for museums; but development is rudimentary. The Department [of Antiquities] has no time to focus on its work" (1999).

Jewelry, coins, statuary, glass, metal, pottery—the collection is of the highest quality. But the visitor can have difficulty understanding or interpreting the objects, as a chronological display pattern is hard to follow. Although many items are not labeled at all, general text information appears on nearby pillars. Here one can gaze on eight-thousand-year-old plaster statuary from 'Ain Ghazal that are some of the earliest human figures ever discovered, and appreciate the distinctively thin pottery of the Nabataeans. In a small room there is also a display of Dead Sea Scrolls.

The Englishman G. Lankester Harding has been credited with founding the museum while he was director of the Department of Antiquities. The government at the time felt it was important to establish a museum that focused on the history of civilization in the East Bank of the kingdom, balancing the collections of the West Bank in the Rockefeller Museum in Jerusalem and helping to promote visits to Amman.

The museum can represent both the pride and the problems of Jordan's government-sponsored museums. On the one hand, the facility is filled with treasures, ready and available to be appreciated—and on the other, the institution has overflowing cairns of objects in need of professional care, identification, and interpretation.

Siham Balqar, former curator at the museum, stated: "Much attention must be paid to permanent collections, whether they are on display or in storage, by improving environmental conditions, and registering and cataloging objects to provide information about them. Therefore collection maintenance, management and conservation are among the most demanding functions for all museums" (Balqar and Zayyat 1994, 156). She also commented that the lighting should be improved by a new electrical network at the museum, and she argued for a new museum in the future: "For a future new museum building, the architect, designer and conservator should cooperate with curators and the museum staff in order to make the museum presentation fully informative and attractive" (Balqar and Zayyat 1994, 156). Finally, she lamented the lack of storage areas for the vast collection; what was once adequate storage under the museum is now overcrowded. With the many successful excavation programs going on throughout the country that provide more and more objects, collections management and storage are a pressing problem.

In addition to these physical problems, there is the absence of library or research facilities, or workshops for installation display, as well as a laboratory for photography and conservation. The most immediate need voiced by the director and the curators was for computerized documentation of the collections (Atyyat 1998).

The installation has changed little from my visits in the 1980s, although new pieces are added occasionally. A meeting with the director, Taysir Atyyat, served to underscore the needs of this flagship institution. With twenty-two years of experience in archeology, he provided frustrated commentary about the management, inventory controls, and operation of the museum. This frustration, shared by other administrators and curators, affected production, creativity, and initiative. Atyyat would be leaving to teach at a university in two months. Many other administrators have left to return to teaching or research.

In his cluttered office, books, papers, files, and records were strewn on tables, and boxes of shards sat on the floor. On the table beside his desk sat a computer and printer. The computer did not work. This was not an isolated example, for although computers had been issued to many of the museums in Jordan, they sat dark and inoperative on desks for lack of parts, software, and training.

The new acting director for the museum is Ahmad Ajajj, who has a master's degree from the University of Jordan in archeology.

Three women work at the museum as curators. All are graduates of the University of Jordan's archeology program. The bachelor's degree includes a course on museum operation that is taught by an archeologist. The women have broad curatorial responsibilities including interpretation, security, and interaction with the public, but not research and publication. From their interviews, lack of specific job descriptions and specific projects for the operation of their museum seemed to inhibit their personal growth and professional achievement. Wishing to remain anonymous, one curator, when asked what her biggest challenge in museum work was, responded: "There is no challenge."

Persistence and Patronage: The Jordan National Gallery

Wijdan Ali is a "restless militant force for the recognition of the contribution of Islamic culture and civilization to the world's patrimony."

—The Star *1999*

Stirrings of desire for a museum of contemporary art that would proudly display the fine arts of a growing cadre of artists from Jordan prompted initial discussions to take place among artists and arts activists early in the 1970s. At one time, Princess Muna, wife of King Hussein, became involved (S. Zaru 1999). In 1972, under her patronage, an arts week was planned to gain support for the building of a new museum. Arts Week activities took place at several sites in Amman, including the Intercontinental Hotel. Featured were performing arts programs, fashion, an exhibition of Nabataean jewelry from the Jordan Archeological Museum, mosaics from the Museum of Popular Traditions (both organized by Wijdan Ali), and a ball. Princess Muna's participation ended with her divorce from the king. Arts Week was a limited success financially, but it served to draw attention to the arts and the need for a museum of fine arts.

In the mid-1970s, the project lost its momentum without clear leadership. Then in 1977–78, interest and energy were renewed by a committee including Wijdan Ali, Samia Zaru, and a few others who began enthusiastically reviving the project. In 1979, the Royal Society of Fine Arts was formally established under the patronage of Queen Noor. The society, under the leadership of Ali, had as its sole purpose the establishment of a national gallery and was to be governed by a board of trustees of not less than nine nor more than fifteen members. The inaugural brochure listed Queen Noor as the patron and a board that included three women: Barbara Attallah, Wijdan Ali, and Samia Zaru. It also listed the society's aims and goals:

· The establishment of the Jordan National Gallery of Fine Arts;
· The patronage of contemporary art in Jordan, the Arab countries and Third World countries;
· Publication and translation of books and research in different branches of Islamic and Arabic culture;
· Exchange of exhibitions between the Gallery and other museums and cultural organizations;

· Providing financial assistance and moral support to artists in Jordan;
· Securing art scholarships for them and holding exhibitions both within and outside Jordan;
· Organizing and participating in seminars, conferences and symposiums pertaining to art and culture within and outside Jordan;
· Founding a reference library on Islamic and international art, and architecture;
· Arranging art competitions and presenting awards to artists on the local and international level;
· Developing artistic education and awareness in Jordan;
· Cooperation with government and private bodies in Jordan in order to enhance the art movement. (Royal Society of Fine Arts 1980)

The society had big dreams. Its major goal was to build a museum with the financial support of businesses, government agencies, embassies, NGOs, research institutions, and private donors. Its members envisioned armies of volunteers, classrooms of schoolchildren, and visitors and eager artists wishing to donate to the permanent collection—but they met with initial disappointment. Although fund-raising efforts were limited and support inconsistent, the planning, ideas, and dreams continued. What the dedicated founders were bucking was not only the lack of a tradition of support for the fine arts, but also a distrust of contemporary visual art based on lack of familiarity and comprehension. This was reinforced by paucity of visual arts training from the primary schools to the universities, limited Ministry of Culture visual arts programs, and the scarcity of well-known and respected indigenous artists.

From its beginning, the museum was planned to showcase contemporary art by Arab and Islamic artists, with a focus on publications, and to set professional standards for collections care, exhibitions, interpretation, and documentation. The educational programs of the museum, however, were slow to take place. Zaru acknowledged: "We were aware of the concept of 'the museum as educator,' but our immediate goal was to establish a collection" (S. Zaru 1999). They wanted to do it all—immediately—but in reality, they had to focus on the establishment of a collection.

Funding has always been an issue in the development of the Jordan National Gallery, just as it is with museums worldwide. A plaque by the front entrance credits the organizations, corporations, and individuals who initially pledged their support. According to the director of the gallery, Rasmi Hamzeh (1998), the government, through the Ministry of Culture, contributes six thousand Jordanian dinars annually, and several banks provide their sponsorship. In addition, foreign embassies and cultural centers underwrite exhibitions and exchanges and help promote and augment the gallery's collection. The United States has contributed through its USAID program, donating a printing press that is shared with and kept at Darat al Funun.

Just as museums in the United States continue to assess their audience, their constituency, their patrons, and their purpose, the gallery attempts to do the same. Museum leaders in Jordan might be comforted by the 1910 *Directory of American Museums* that addressed the creation of American museums with these words:

> Museums are not born of definite educational or recreational intent as often as they are of the moods of hobby-riding collectors, of self-centered enthusiasts and of the memorial-seeking rich. Perhaps this is well. The world needs variety more than it needs standards. There can be no standards in museums. Museums must be born of enthusiasm and grow through unselfish devotion; and enthusiasm and unselfish devotion must be permitted to choose their own objectives and their own methods. (Dana 1917, 22)

Initially, Ali found that not many women were interested in the museum project, but many men were. Those women who were supportive were often artists and included gallery director Nuha Batchone, founder of The Gallery at the Intercontinental Hotel in Amman. Many of the women she contacted were not interested in modern, contemporary, or abstract art; their taste was for Orientalist and European art. Ali's success in enthusing and fund-raising was hard won: "At social functions women would come up to me and ask: 'And how is the art?' along with [asking] how were my children. Did they think I founded the National Gallery to amuse myself?" (Ali 1999).

Well aware of the activities, fund-raising events, and incentives that other museums in Europe and the United States use to garner support, enlarge audiences, and develop member groups, Ali's attempts to start a membership campaign did not meet with success. "What could we offer members that they wouldn't already get for free?" (Ali 1999). Jordanians can visit free of charge, and the warm, fuzzy feeling of doing something good for cultural development was not enough to instigate a profitable membership program. Although donations to the gallery were deductible under Jordanian tax law, there were few contemporary artists in Jordan whose work was museum quality, few collectors of contemporary Arab or Islamic art who had collections to give, and fewer activists who might spearhead patron groups or collector clubs.

With these difficulties in mind, the founding board of the museum scaled down their big dreams and began to search for a facility in which they could start out small. Site selection was very important; they wanted the museum to be accessible by public transportation, to be in a quiet neighborhood, and to have affordable rent. They found such a facility on Jebel Weibde in Amman, facing a small park and near a major bus and transportation center—the residence of Raouf Abu Jabir, an art connoisseur and collector. The location was excellent, but there were difficulties adapting the rented building to a museum, for the rooms were small and had low ceilings. Board members could recall the original house plan long after it became a museum, jokingly referring to the location of works of art as if they hung in the kitchen or in the bedroom.

In an article on the renovations and additions to the gallery, architect Jafar Tukan makes his challenge clear: "The lower floor, which is to receive the addition, is a villa rather crudely transformed to serve as a Gallery of Art" (1984, 46).

Now built up to four floors, the gallery spaces have been augmented and expanded. Lighting, security, storage, and climate controls are part of the professional renovation and design. In 1980 the gallery opened with seventy-five works of art in the collection. Today, it boasts a sixteen-hundred-piece collection of paintings, sculpture, ceramics, and graphics representative of Brunei, Indonesia, Pakistan, and Iran to the east, Turkey, the Gulf and the Levant, and the North African Maghreb to the west. Initially the collection included Orientalist paintings by such artists as Gérôme, Compte de Nouy, Ernst, Roberts, and Eugene Delacroix. These works were later deaccessioned, and funds from their sale were used to purchase the building in 1993. Their initial inclusion in the museum collection might be explained by their availability for donation and the prevailing taste of patrons.

The collection of contemporary art grew from purchases, donations by Jordanian artists and collectors, and collection exchanges between other museums, galleries, and international artists who were invited to exhibit. By 1982, twenty-three women artists from the Mashreq, Maghreb, and Turkey were represented in the four-hundred-piece permanent collection (Ali 1984, 28).

Although the Jordan National Gallery grew from the support of many, Ali, as president of the Royal Society of Fine Arts, is credited as the founder, the catalyst who solidified ideas and dreams into reality. Jalal Uddin Ahmed, editor of *Arts and the Islamic World* magazine, addresses her importance:

> Herself a practicing painter and an avid and discerning collector of the work of contemporary artists, [Princess Wijdan Ali] has helped to establish and develop the Jordan National Art Gallery as one of the finest collections of the work of Jordanian artists as well as those from many other countries of the Islamic world from Morocco to Indonesia. In that sense it is a pilot project of immense significance which can serve as a model for many other countries in that vast area where facilities for viewing the whole range of work being done by the artists even in the neighboring countries of the Islamic world are still far from accurate. (Ahmed 1984, 6)

Between 1980 and 1994, the gallery presented eighty-two exhibitions. Many were group and one-person shows of Jordanian artists. Others were traveling exhibits from major museums in the United States, Europe, and the Arab world including the Centre Pompidou, Paris, the Harvard Semitic Museum, Massachusetts, the Ankara State Museum, Turkey, the Musée d'art et d'histoire, Switzerland, the Victoria and Albert Museum, London, the Mahmoud Mokhtar Museum, Cairo, the Belvedere Museum, Tunisia, and the Iraqi Contemporary Art Museum, Baghdad. The permanent collection of the gallery has been shown in many countries in Europe, the United States, and other Middle Eastern countries.

Hopes for a cadre of volunteer women who would assist in the operation, act as docents, and actively serve on the board of trustees were not immediately realized. Volunteerism in Jordan (excluding times of war or resistance) for activities outside the home has usually been directed toward hospitals and health care and toward the education of other women.

The first director of the National Gallery was artist Samir Tabbaa. Following him, the gallery was administered by Suhail Bisharat, a practicing artist, trained in geology. Presently the director, a graduate of the Institute of Diplomacy in Amman, is Rasmi Hamzeh. He focuses on administrative and fund-raising activities, while Wijdan Ali oversees curatorial affairs. Ali's advice to young women who are just entering the museum field epitomizes her optimism and reflects her hard work: "Be perseverant. Don't lose hope. Expect many disappointments, but the end result is worth it" (1999).

The Jordan National Gallery has grown from a compartmented suburban home to a four-story visual arts complex that has space for traveling shows, a permanent collection, lectures, seminars, performances, a coffee shop, gift shop, offices, library, and storage areas. The exhibit schedule of 1999 reflected the diversity of its programs:

- Pakistani exhibition
- Contemporary Armenian art
- Spanish exhibition
- Exhibition of Muhanna Durra
- Exhibition of Faisal Samra and Hussein Sherief
- Exhibition of Ernestine Ruben
- Jordanian-Spanish art exhibition

The Janus Has Many Faces: Museum of Jordanian Heritage

I like the museum just like my children.

—*Mohammad Hatamleh*

From the beginning, the idea of the museum was there, and the space was there, although not the one you see today.

—*Seteney Shami*

The Museum of Jordanian Heritage at Yarmouk University was established in 1984 as part of the Institute of Archeology and Anthropology with the support of the Jordanian Department of Antiquities, the University of Leiden, the Universities of San Diego and Nevada, Tübingen University, the Free University of Berlin, and the French National Center for Scientific Research. Creation of the museum and its first exhibition took four years— Queen Noor formally opened it in 1988. In the inaugural catalog, credit for support is given to Herwig Bartels, ambassador of the Federal Republic of Germany to Jordan. Also credited with assistance by the director of the Institute of Archaeology and Anthropology, Moawiyah Ibrahim, are Widad Kawar, connoisseur, author, collector of costumes, and textiles, and Ammar Khammash, the designer and building consultant who had transformed the Darat al Funun in Amman.

"At the beginning, there were no staff that were hired for the museum specifically, although lots of people worked on it" (Shami 1999). Moawiyah Ibrahim is credited with having the energy to marshal the necessary resources; however, two women stand out as important in the museum's development. Foremost is the first curator, Birgit Mershen, an anthropologist who spent eight years at Yarmouk University. Her dedication to the museum was evident from the beginning: "We started working on the establishment of the museum in 1984. Our collections then consisted of the finds of the Institute's excavations. That year Yarmouk University provided small sums of money to start our ethnographic collection. I vividly remember how we enthusiastically registered the first handful of objects" (Mershen 1988, 14).

Another woman, Jordanian anthropologist Seteney Shami, helped to plan the museum, as a member of the development committee from 1984 to 1986. She also worked on the text and the layout of the exhibits. An author, educator, and consultant, she has had extensive field experience in Jordan, Turkey, and the Caucasus, and is presently program director at the Social Science Research Council in New York City.

Foreign institutions continue to support the museum financially and professionally, conducting research and excavations that augment the museum's exhibits. The goals of the museum reflect international participation:

- Studying and documenting the human heritage of Jordan;
- Conservation and restoration of all of its materials;
- Building cultural bridges with international society; and
- Helping researchers and academic specialists.

The museum "accomplish[es] these goals by cooperating with local institutions, universities, schools, the Ministry of Education and Ministry of Culture, international universities and museums; by setting up exhibits, meetings, and lectures; and by publishing, and presenting training programs and workshops" (Hatamleh 1998b).

The museum serves as a showcase for the arts, crafts, and history of Jordan. The chronological exhibits of prehistory through the Ottoman period portray the sequence of historical eras in a way that develops Jordan's relationship to former civilizations and confirms its present identity through them. As Mershen explains, "The present is nothing but the—momentarily—latest development; today's present is nothing but tomorrow's past" (1988, 13). The museum presentation reflects correlations between natural, demographic, socioeconomic, and cultural facts in a blending of archeological and ethnographic exhibits. The exhibits focus on how Jordan evolved from prehistory, then reflect on Jordan's future.

Maffi proposes that Jordan's museums have been actively involved in the creation of a new national cultural identity, and this museum serves as a good example. In *Jordanies*, she posits that Jordanian museums present a direct link between contemporary and ancient civilizations, referencing how the Museum of Jordanian Heritage stresses historical connections and the usage of the term Jund al-Urdun for the first time by the Umayyads (Maffi 1999, 95). This in turn lays the philosophical, moral, and physical groundwork for future Hashemite legitimacy.

As a participant in the development of the museum, Shami adds that it represents a negotiated product. There were many voices in its development, and often there were clashes between archeologists and anthropologists in their approach. Some wanted the museum to cater to a tourist audience; others wanted it primarily as an educational institution focusing on community outreach, lectures, and ongoing active research in oral history. In the end both audiences were served, but not as well as either side had hoped. Eventually, even the name of the museum was deliberately chosen to be ambiguous and to be inclusive of all the heritages of Jordan (Shami 1999).

Former director Ibrahim considered the museum the "first attempt at a pedagogical museum in our country. It displays our archeological and cultural heritage in a proper manner and gives our citizens and visitors, from all ages and walks of life, the opportunity to appreciate Jordan's cultural heritage and its valuable contribution to human civilization" (Ibrahim 1988, 11).

As a good classical Janus should, the museum meets the educational needs of the community as well as those of the university. It prepares workshops for schoolchildren, going outside the museum into classrooms and using objects to show how things like stone carvings, pottery, and textiles were made and used in the past. Museum staff design educational programs for schoolchildren in cooperation with the regional office of the Ministry of Education, and an Association of Friends of the Museum was founded that acts as a public awareness liaison to the community. Mershen viewed the museum as having many faces and serving many needs: "a place of learning in an enjoyable atmosphere, a place of recreation and of social activity, in addition to its research function" (1988, 12).

A third face for the museum, one that occasionally provoked a grimace, was that of tourist attraction. Certainly everyone wanted a museum of international prestige, but in the end it was decided not to focus on this. Shami (1999) commented that the differences of opinion on the committee were "scholarly, disciplinary, conceptual . . . and not based on personalities or power struggles. The consensus was the museum would and should be interesting for tourists, but these could also be local tourists, or Arab tourists from the region as well as Western tourists."

In addition to its permanent displays, the museum also contains a temporary exhibit hall for traveling exhibits as well as for short-term displays of newly excavated material. These exhibits serve to maintain interest in the museum's vibrancy and afford hands-on exhibit development and lending experience in cultural exchanges with other museums and scholars.

Many in Jordan consider this museum to be Jordan's finest because of the professional and state-of-the-art display techniques, and also perhaps because its sophisticated presentation tells a story Jordanians want to hear.

Traditions on Parade: Museum of Popular Traditions

> Jordanian culture today is a cumulative repository of successive human traditions, practices and beliefs that must be measured in millennia.
>
> —*Queen Noor*

The candid opening sentence in an early 1970s brochure on the Museum of Popular Traditions states that the museum "is a modest attempt to revive the national heritage." Targeting the youth of the country, the brochure further states the museum should "bring certainty to the minds of the people of this country . . . that their homeland is of genuine origin, that their nation is of noble descent and that they have their own identity" (Al Tel, n.d).

The idea for this museum of national heritage is credited to Sa'adieh Al

Tel, who began collecting for the institution in Jerusalem in 1965 in Souk Kutaneen with a committee that was chaired by the governor of that city. After the 1967 war with Israel, she and the collection moved to Amman, where she founded the Jordan Folklore Club, then the museum, where she became director. Although she worked closely with governmental agencies, she was never an employee and always remained a volunteer. Widad Kawar (1999) recalled this strong, dedicated woman: "Sa'adieh gave people style in Jordan. She was a lady of taste." She loved honey, and kept a peacock and an ostrich in her garden.

Al Tel credited her husband, Wasfi Tel (then Jordan's prime minister), for encouraging her in the project, and indeed his high government position afforded support for the establishment of the museum at the Roman Theater in downtown Amman and the clout to have financial requests and fiscal independence judiciously implemented.

The museum facility, formerly the offices for the Department of Antiquities, was renovated twice, once for the inaugural opening in the 1970s and then again in 1980. Its location, on the left side of the entrance to the theater, is both an asset and a problem—an asset in terms of its prime real estate and access for visitors, and a problem because of the environmental conditions existing outside (urban pollution) and inside (light, climate control, and space limitations). In the five halls of the museum, the costume exhibits are divided geographically by East and West Bank, featuring Palestinian costume and headdresses, jewelry, and household items (including baskets, weavings, and utensils). In the lower chamber, there is a small collection of Byzantine mosaics.

Traditionally the museum employed an exhibit designer. Initially it was Patrick Cuman; later, Ali Jabri, nephew of the director, assumed the responsibility. This professional approach to museum exhibit design has brought life to the cloth, metal, and stone on display. The exhibits are accessible and attractive, and many are well documented. Text panels augment displays with historical information, in Arabic and English, and photographs provide context.

Further distinctions set this museum apart from other government museums: the museum maintains its own separate budget, and funds from the entrance fee can be put back into the museum budget to satisfy immediate needs or projects. It is in this way that a new brochure will be funded. Additionally, the museum's charter named Al Tel the director of the museum as well as the curator. This unique situation was honored until she left, then the administrative system by which all other government museums operate was adopted.

Al Tel was personally involved in choosing objects for the permanent collection. She negotiated sales and documented the donations and purchases. She secured many costumes as donations before funds were released for their purchase from the government. Even after the museum was established in Amman, villagers from throughout the country who needed money came to her in order to sell their costumes and jewelry. Al Tel was assisted by two other women, Muna Zaglow and Hidea Abaza.

Waf'a Tel (1998), sister-in-law of Sa'adieh Al Tel, recalled her involvement with the museum. "Our original purpose was to collect the things we loved—and we wanted to hold a fashion show. The costumes we collected from Madaba and Irbid were given to us out of trust and love. Later when we had our collections, then the government helped."

Early collecting for the museum was fun but potentially dangerous. Waf'a Tel described the joy of her trips even when the country was in the midst of civil war—when Palestinians and Jordanians were fighting each other and travel was often unsafe. On one occasion, she and several other women drove south from Amman to the town of Madaba—a three-hour drive—in their small Volkswagen to look for objects for the museum. There, a schoolteacher, Nuha Karachi, took them personally to homes where they solicited donations. All along the way she and the other women sang as they drove, unafraid (Tel 1998).

Nine women worked on the committee with Sa'adieh Al Tel, helping to develop the museum: Awalif Sharihah, Haifa Shariah, Jan Merza, Haya Abu Khoura, Khowla Abu Khoura, Jenwa Madi, and Sofa Khalti. They held their first fund-raiser in 1970, a fashion show at Sports City in Amman. They attempted to give the profits to King Hussein as a wedding present, but the king refused the donation, and the money raised was given to Sports City (Tel 1998).

In 1986, four years before Al Tel resigned for health reasons, Huda Kilani was appointed curator at the museum. A graduate in archeology from the University of Jordan, she had been assisting at the museum since 1983. Today, one of Kilani's main concerns for the museum is better collections management and computerized documentation of the collection (Kilani 1999a). The present system uses a handwritten ledger and large index cards that show inventory number, title, media, date or period, how the object was acquired, description, size, and origin and contains a space for a photograph. Currently under discussion among museum curators is whether they should develop their own inventory system or be part of a larger nationwide system coordinated by the Department of Antiquities. Another project in process is a new brochure.

The museum, like others in Amman, has changed its policies in order to capitalize on the growing tourist market. The entrance fee has been increased from 250 fils to one Jordanian dinar for foreign visitors; the museum is now open seven days a week (formerly it was closed on Tuesdays), and summer hours have been extended until five P.M.

There are no written acquisition and deaccession policies for the museum. For such activities, the museum seeks advice from the Ministry of Tourism and Antiquities. The curator does not participate directly in long-range planning for the museum and presently has no official job description (Kilani 1998). Concerning evaluation of her job performance, she credits the director of the Department of Antiquities for knowing what she is doing from the reports and requests she sends him. She has not asked to see her annual reviews that are sent to the Ministry of Civil Service Workers.

The Price of History:
Numismatic Museum, Central Bank of Jordan

Art has a common denominator: Virtue, good taste, noble feelings and generosity are values from which the fine arts flow.

—*Ministry of Culture*

How civilizations develop, use, and design their money tells us a great deal about them. Coinage provides information for reconstructing the history of the civilizations that minted them. The peoples who ruled the area we call Jordan today left their legacy through coins and objects of monetary value, examples of which can be seen in the Numismatic Museum of the Central Bank of Jordan in Amman. Coins become part of our material culture by documenting the religions, politics, commerce, and daily life of the past.

Collecting for the Numismatic Museum began as early as 1982; the former governor of the bank, Hussein Kassim, opened the museum, and King Hussein dedicated it in 1988. The museum's collection includes coinage, paper money, and Hashemite commemorative medals.

Zahida Safer, the present curator, studied at the Sorbonne, University of Paris, and did her dissertation on the monuments of Petra. Formerly employed by the Department of Antiquities, her interests have focused on the study of alphabets and inscriptions, including Latin, Nabataean, and Arabic.

Adults and scholars can make an appointment to visit, however, the importance that the museum places on students and education is apparent in the introductory reception area it has provided for school groups. Students visit at the beginning of the school year, from September through November, then return after the rains in April and May. They arrive through a separate walkway from the street into an entrance hall whose wall murals and graphics depict medieval money making. They are greeted by an introductory video presentation on the history of money. Tours of the large one-room museum begin at the left of the entrance with well-labeled and lighted cases containing coinage presented chronologically from the Ptolemaic period. Visitors progress clockwise through periods, dynasties, and kingdoms, through the Ottoman and Mandate periods to contemporary Hashemite times. This is one of the few museums in Jordan where the Ottoman and Mandate periods are included as a full participant in Jordan's history. Reproductions of artwork on the walls of the room depict the story of coinage throughout the ages.

There are presently 2,385 pieces in the collection; among them 28 Nabataean, 112 Roman, 80 Byzantine, and approximately 240 early Islamic examples. There is no fixed annual budget. The goal of the museum is to obtain full coverage of coinage used in the area, and accessions are requested from the board of the bank on an individual basis.

The contemporary collections include examples of all currency minted or printed for the country since 1949, as well as commemorative medals recognizing state visits, such as the first visit of a pope, and important political, monarchal, and historical events.

Women are represented in the ancient coinage of the Greek and Roman empires and on the Nabataean coins depicting Aretas IV, the king of Petra, who had two wives. The collection contains one coin depicting each wife. Contemporary Jordanian coins bear the bust, in profile, of King Hussein; early bills represent the young King Hussein in a Western business suit; later bills represent King Hussein in more than one type of attire—both in the Bedouin traditional headdress and bareheaded in Western attire. There are no contemporary images of women on Jordanian currency.

A Taste of Salt: Salt Folklore Museum

We need to find ways to make people know about our museum. Maybe because we are so close to Amman we are unknown.

—*Raida Al Haliq*

Originally begun in 1983, then dedicated at a downtown site by King Hussein in 1987, the Salt Folklore Museum has occupied the top floor of the restored Tukan villa since 1997. This impressive stone villa, which at one time served as a school, also houses the Museum of Archeology on the first floor and the Folklore Museum and the offices of the Salt Archeological Department on the second floor.

Unlike many other government museums, admittance is free, and the majority of employees and volunteers are women. According to curator Muasar Audeh Hadidi (1999), there are ten women involved in all aspects of the museum operation. Hadidi received her bachelor of arts degree in history and began working with museums in 1983. She works with her husband, director of the Salt Archeological Office.

Currently, the Folklore Museum presents two exhibit themes at its location on the second floor of the villa: Bedouin and village life. In the village exhibit room, models depict women and the household objects they use in domestic life, such as kitchen implements and tools for food grinding, cooking, and storage. Bedding and personal grooming items are displayed, along with a wall-mounted, embroidered woman's costume from Salt containing some twenty meters of material, often up to 3.5 meters in length as well. The other exhibit room features male mannequins in various attitudes of repose and hospitality. The original colorful tiles on the floor of the rooms and the wood-framed case windows remind the visitor of the origins of this villa, built circa 1892. Little didactic material is available for visitor interpretation, and most objects and settings are without labels.

Discussion with the curator and other staff reveals their concern for enlivening the museum. Although their general goals are to make the museum better known, their more immediate goal is to create policies that support the female staff in the work environment. Hadidi believes the museum's greatest need is in preservation of metal and organic materials. Raida Al Haliq, the financial administrator for the museum and an enthusiastic spokesperson, also gives tours to visitors and students. Haliq (1999) says that the museum suffers from an image problem and would benefit from creative ways to advertise its services. The proximity of Salt to Amman impacts negatively, as organized tours tend to focus on the capital and the major sites of Jerash and Petra, bypassing Salt. Further, she states that there are no amenities such as first-class hotels or restaurants in Salt to attract tourists. She suggests that radio and TV advertising could increase the museum's attendance, and this might also help bring in local residents.

Biographies, Founders to Patrons

Who are some of the women founders and what are their institutions? In Amman: Hidea Abaza, the Folklore Museum; Wijdan Ali, the Jordan National Gallery; Aida Naghawi, the Islamic Museum; Suha Shoman, the Darat al Funun; and Sa'adieh Al Tel, the Jordan Museum of Popular Traditions. In Ma'an: Nazmieh Rida Tawfiq Darwish, who founded the King Abdullah Museum. Several other women stand out as important in the development of museums—women who have served on committees, raised funds, and donated their time and talents. Among them are gallery owner Nuha Batchone, collector Widad Kawar, artist/arts activist Hind Nasser, Queen Noor, artist/arts educator Samia Zaru, and artist/teacher Fahrelnissa Zeid. There are also several women whose past service has not often received public attention, including Rajwa bint Ali, Naeimeh Asfour, Muna Deeb, and Muna Zaglow.

Among the many cultural arts advocates in Jordan, the following eleven women have played major active and influential roles in the development and operation of Jordan's museums.

Hidea Abaza: Museum Founder, Curator

Born in Zarqa, Jordan, Hidea Abaza is credited as the founder of the Folklore Museum located at the Roman Theater in downtown Amman, and the first curator for the Department of Antiquities. First trained as a lawyer, she received her master of arts degree from Leicester University in England with a specialty in museums, law, and antiquities. For many years, while working for the Department of Antiquities, she helped build the Folklore Museum's collections by personally going to villages to purchase items. She has also been credited for initiating the regional approach to museum development in Jordan. In 1983 she left the Folklore Museum to practice law, dividing her time between Amman and Zarqa.

Khairieh Amr: Director, Directorate of Museums, Archeologist, Author

Born in 1956, Khairieh Amr received her doctorate in archeology from the London Institute of Archeology at the University of London and worked as the assistant to the director of excavations at the Department of Antiquities. Until recently she was a field archaeologist, objects interpreter, supervisor of site protection, and editor of archeological journals. She then assumed the directorship of the newly created Directorate of Museums at the Department of Antiquities. Her publications include *The Pottery from Petra: A Neutron Activation Analysis Study* and more than fifty articles in archeological journals about archaeological work in Jordan.

HRH Princess Wijdan Ali: Art Historian, Curator, Museum Founder, Painter, Author

Born in 1939, Wijdan Ali received her bachelor of arts degree from Beirut College for Women and her master of arts degree and doctorate in Islamic art from the School of Oriental and African Studies at the University of London. She founded the Jordan National Gallery in 1980 and is responsible for its curatorial direction. She has taught Islamic civilization at the Institute of Diplomacy and was head of the research department, vice president of the institute, and dean of the University of Jordan. She was the first woman to enter the Ministry of Foreign Affairs in Jordan and the first woman diplomat to represent Jordan at the United Nations. She has written more than seventeen publications, has curated many international exhibitions, has had twenty-one one-person exhibitions, and has participated in fifty-two group exhibitions. Her public recognition includes an award from the International Council of Women in the Arts; the Al-Hussein bin Talal Gold Medal for Artistic Achievement; recognition as Officier de l'Ordre des Arts et des Lettres by the French Ministry of Culture; and the Diplome d'Honneur from the Institut Européen de Science Humaine dans la Discipline Academique Beaux Arts, Brussels, Belgium.

Siham Balqar: Curator, Museum Administrator

Born in Amman, Jordan, in 1945, Siham Balqar received her bachelor of arts degree in archeology from the University of Jordan, then continued her education in Holland, England, and Germany. In 1969 she held the positions of director and curator of the Archeological Museum at the Citadel in Amman. She has organized several international traveling exhibitions of Jordanian antiquities throughout the years. An AAM museum personnel exchange program (IPAM) allowed her to continue graduate work at Harvard University's Semitic Museum. Now retired, she acts as a volunteer and a mentor to employees in the Department of Antiquities and is helping to prepare a new guidebook for the Archeological Museum.

Nazmieh Rida Tawfiq Darwish: Museum Founder, Curator, Department Administrator, Author

Born in Amman, Jordan in 1945, Nazmieh Rida Tawfiq Darwish was the first female archeologist in the kingdom, receiving her bachelor of arts degree in archeology from the University of Jordan. Initially she worked for the Department of Antiquities as a curator and inspector of archeology. She received her master's degree through an eighteen-month USAID scholarship to study museums and national parks in the United States, taking courses through the Smithsonian Institution, the Oriental Institute, the National Park Service, the Natural History Museum, and Columbia University in Missouri, finally receiving her master of arts degree in anthropology and archeology at the University of Utah. She received additional training in conservation studies in Rome. She was the organizer of the International Conference on the History and Archeology of Jordan since 1980, and she wrote the guidebook for the Jordan Archeological Museum and a tourist guidebook, *Jordan*. After working in the Excavations Department and starting the Awareness Program for children, she is now director of cultural and public relations for the Department of Antiquities.

Widad Kawar: Arts Patron, Collector, Author

Born in Bethlehem, Palestine, in 1932, Widad Kawar received her bachelor of arts degree in history from Beirut College for Women and the American

University of Beirut, then continued her graduate studies at Arizona State University in archeology and anthropology. An authority on Palestinian textiles and costumes, she has authored and coauthored several books and articles. As owner of the Widad Kawar Arab Heritage Collection of Palestinian and Arab Costumes, a documented collection of more than one thousand embroidered costumes and accessories, she makes her collection available for research to scholars. She participates with cultural organizations, often serving on boards as an advisor.

Aida Naghawi: Museum Founder, Curator, Department Administrator

Born in Amman, Jordan, in 1952, Aida Naghawi graduated from the University of Jordan with a bachelor of arts degree in archeology. In 1996, she established the Islamic Museum at the King Abdullah Mosque in Amman. She was the first curator of the Jerash museum and the first woman antiquities inspector and director of an archeological site. Presently she is an administrator at the Department of Antiquities and is assisting in the establishment of the Abu-Ubida Museum in the Jordan Valley.

Suha Shoman: Museum Founder, Arts Patron, Arts Administrator, Artist, Author

Born in Jerusalem, Palestine, in 1944, Suha Shoman studied law in Beirut and at the Sorbonne in Paris. Active as a patron of the arts for many years, in 1993 she founded the Abdul Hameed Shoman Foundation's Darat al Funun, a visual and performing arts center funded by the Arab Bank. It is now under the umbrella of the Khalid Shoman foundation. Under her leadership, the facility grew to include galleries, workshops, and a library, and presents exhibitions, films, concerts, lectures, and seminars. A student at the Fahrelnissa Zeid Royal Institute of Fine Arts, she studied under Fahrelnissa Zeid and is a prolific painter. Her paintings often reflect the landscape environment of Petra. She has exhibited widely in Europe, at the Galerie Wally Findlay, Galerie P. Morda, and annually at the Salon d'Automne in Paris; in London at the Barbican Centre; and in Canada, the United States, and in Jordan. Her works are in many private and museum collections.

Sa'adieh Al Tel: Museum Founder, Administrator, Curator, Author

Born in 1915 in Syria, Sa'adieh Al Tel received no formal postsecondary education. Her name is recorded several ways in publications: Sadiyeh, Saadiyé, and Sa'adiyeh, in addition to Sa'adieh. She lived in Jerusalem for several years where she began collecting Palestinian village costumes, hoping to start a museum there. Moving to Amman after the 1967 war with Israel, she founded the Museum of Popular Traditions downtown at the Roman Theater in 1971. Those who worked with her described her as an intelligent, strong, self-confident woman, dedicated to the museum. She died in 1998.

Samia Zaru: Painter, Sculptor, Art Educator, Author

Born in Nablus, Palestine, in 1938, Samia Zaru graduated from the American University of Beirut, then continued with her graduate studies at the Corcoran School of Art and Design and the American University in Washington, D.C. As an art educator she has provided in-service training for teachers, developed the art curriculum for UNRWA in Palestine, and served as an art and design curriculum expert for the Jordanian Ministry of Education, the Palestine Art Curriculum Committee, the government of Yemen, and the World Bank. She is an educator, art instructor, and lecturer at many institutions. Active in the arts and cultural arena in Jordan, she has served on many museum committees, including the founding committees of the Jordan National Gallery and the Jordan Artists Association. In the 1960s she had a retrospective in Palestine. She has received honors and prizes in Jordan and Iraq, and a bronze medal for sculpture at the International Festival of Creativity in Cairo. She has exhibited widely in the Middle East, Europe, and the United States and is represented in many private, corporate, and museum collections.

HRH Princess Fahrelnissa Zeid: Painter, Sculptor, Art Teacher, Author

Born in Istanbul in 1901, Fahrelnissa Zeid (Fahr El Nissa Zeid) studied at the Academy of Fine Arts in Istanbul from 1920 to 1923, then at the

Académie Ranson in Paris. Her paintings and sculpture were exhibited in Europe in such galleries as Gimpel and Sons, the St. Georges Gallery, the Institute of Contemporary Art, and Lords Gallery in London—and the Collette Allendy Gallery, Galerie de Beaune, Dina Vierney Gallery, and Katia Granoff Galleries in Paris. Her acrylic sculptures were featured at an exhibit in the Louvre, and her graphic works were shown in museums in the United States in New York City and Cincinnati, and, after her death, in several museums including the National Museum of Women in the Arts in Washington, D.C. The wife of Iraq's Hashemite ambassador to Europe, she lived and worked in Paris, London, and Berlin for years before moving to Amman in 1975. Opening the Fahrelnissa Zeid Royal Institute of Fine Arts, a salon for women painters, she became a major influence in the artistic and cultural development of Jordan through her teaching, support, encouragement, and promotion of artists. Many talented women came briefly into her sphere, including writer Janset Shamey and Samia Zaru, whom she credited as introducing art to Jordanian children. She died in 1991. A major tribute was given to her in 1998 at a symposium where a panel of artists, arts administrators, critics, collectors, and educators discussed her influence and importance.

Conclusion

This book contains many facts about museums and women, but in essence it is a book of questions and insights. Museums in the Middle East have grown in fits and starts since the first ones opened in Turkey. The mission of many of these institutions is changing from being artifact repositories to being places of enlightenment and discovery. They are still evolving—as the need, awareness, and audience demands—striving to keep up with the continuous stream of excavated material in need of protection, contemporary artistic production, and the growing interest in cultural tourism. Museums throughout the Middle East face similar problems; most are government sponsored, and most pursue similar goals. The situation in Jordan is typical.

Many women have chosen a career in museum work in Jordan and are keenly aware of the need for museums to be interpreters and conservers of culture. Antiquities department administrators realize that their facilities are a major tourist asset and revenue source; educators are cognizant of the role that museums can play in developing and promoting cultural identity. But knowing all that, the museums of Jordan remain static. They have not been developed to their fullest potential.

What are some of the broad issues that I observed in Jordan? First, museums are not being used as they could be—either for purposes of education or for economic advantage. Second, although a large percentage of museum personnel were women, these women did not participate in the power structure, and few were involved in the planning and evaluation processes. Third, I saw that the American concept of a "good" museum was not the same as the concepts held by other peoples. I also learned that my training in site and program evaluation was often inappropriate for Jordan, as was my intense American focus on diversity and multiculturalism. Instead, I was made aware of the urgency to establish cohesive internal cultural identity as well as to give external legitimacy to the history of Jordan (a similar situation for other museums of the Levant and Gulf)—the need to forge, not divide identity for this young country composed of diverse ethnic and religious peoples.

These findings do not signal a negation of my dedication to the technical standards called for in proper environmental, statistical, conservational, or social museology; they simply recognize that culture shapes the thinking of other peoples and conditions many of their concepts as well as their behavior. Culture shapes identity, history, life experiences, and what is produced. It is through cultural tools that one envisions the future and defines the concepts of heritage. Defined in those cultural terms, not in the economic terms of its fuel-endowed neighbors, Jordan is one of the richest countries in the world.

What are some of the patterns I found as I visited, interviewed, and observed? What similarities or differences did I find between my case studies in Jordan and my experiences in the United States regarding museums themselves and the lives of the women who work in them? The most obvious similarities are universal. I found the basic professional needs of the museums very much the same, usually following this order: funding, need for better technology, and need for training. The personal needs of the women employees revolved around balancing the demands of home and work. As for the differences among young, female museum workers in government museum employment, I encountered little professional assertiveness, little concern for networking, and little interest in women's career organizations.

What are some specific observations about the museums of Jordan? First, there are only two contemporary art museums (one is a visual and performing arts center that operates much like a museum), five historical museums, and three science museums. The other museums focus on antiquities and ethnography. Like their counterparts in the Levant region, it seems that the Jordanians have not learned public irony or self-mockery yet, for I found no parallels to the Dog Museum as in Kansas City, Missouri, or the Museum of Bad Art as exists in Dedham, Massachusetts. Nor have they developed the luxury of specificity with museums devoted to minority ethnic groups, fads, esoterica, or women.

Second, Jordanian and Palestinian cultural representation is often intertwined, side by side, or fused in explanations of the history of the Jordanian state. In contrast, exhibitions of material culture from modern times that represent Jordan's joint heritage with its neighbors Syria, Iraq, or Saudi Arabia were not well developed.

The museum structure and governance that I am most familiar with—the nonprofit, autonomous, private, educationally focused institution governed by volunteer boards—are the exception in the Middle East. Those private museums and art centers in Jordan that do exist, however, are leaders in their fields, setting standards and achieving goals of international importance. In addition, curators, not directors, managed the day-to-day operation of Jordan's governmentally sponsored museums. The Museum of Popular Traditions was an exception to this. A great many of these curators have been women, and they handle the in-house administrative and curatorial needs of their museums but not necessarily the educational programs. Officially, the director general of antiquities is the director of these archeological, historical, ethnographic, and folkloric museums, and he acts as a board would in setting policy and approving budgets within the system of the Ministry of Tourism and Antiquities.

There is a dilemma for museums concerning their role as educators and historians that became apparent in my research. In Jordan, many people disparage the old-fashioned or tribal way of life they see depicted in their museum exhibition displays. They do not want to identify with such "backward" ways and thus relegate the village or Bedouin lifestyle to their historical past. Yet these ways are very much alive in areas a short drive from Amman and throughout the country. This disassociation is reflected in low museum attendance and lack of interest by many residents.

In a complex reversal, young people brought on school trips from small villages and towns into Amman to visit the major museums often see a reflection of the lives of their grandparents, their parents, or themselves in the ethnographic museums. They confront the confusing situation wherein their village lifestyle is being displayed to tourists as inferior, historic, quaint, or somehow not real. But they know they are still living it.

American museums are usually defined in terms of amenities and programs—then redefined by excellence and equity goals in terms of their educational services. Museum success in Jordan relies heavily on the discovery, excavation, conservation, and identification of art and artifacts and less on educational programming or community interaction and involvement.

Further, it is apparent that the more contemporary the purpose and presentations of museums, the more contemporary the technology is, the more programs presented, and the higher number of indigenous publications produced.

More than one museum administrator in Jordan lamented the lack of tradition in museum going, support, and collecting in their culture. Without this tradition, what can be done to promote museological development? What can energize museums? More money is one answer. Certainly a campaign of awareness—one that would target families, young people, and women as visitors, participants, and volunteers—is another. Media advertising directed toward renewed reverence and respect for the heritage found in museums and coordinated efforts to make museums relevant to the community would be a third. This effort might take the form of youth activities and projects, parent-child afterschool workshops, classes, contests, and clubs. Key components would be the private sector, private enterprise, and neighborhood involvement. But important questions remain: how to best integrate government museums and the private sector—and does the government want these initiatives to develop on their own without careful study and control?

Internally, museum staff could be offered incentives for creative ideas and achievements. Allied to this is the establishment of competition. In most government-operated museums everything is standardized; initiative has little reward—yet the Department of Antiquities knows how semiautonomy for the Museum of Popular Traditions in Amman has enhanced its reputation internationally, its exhibit design, signage, and public interaction.

Related to this is the need for publicity. All media (word of mouth, billboards, television, radio, newspapers, Internet, brochures, etc.) could be used to energize museums. Almost all of the women curators interviewed were working on a brochure or catalog for their museums, and had been for years. But these projects were stifled for many reasons. What incentive did the curators have to publish? Prestige and professionalism? Individualism, peer competition, and professional aggrandizement or promotion are not necessarily rewarded. What incentive did the Department of Antiquities have to publish brochures? Publications cost money and budgets remain low. Further, funds realized from the sale of publications would not go back to the museums themselves or to the department, but into ministry budgets.

What incentives could be offered to initiate museum publications, pro-

grams, and development? Semiautonomy and direct access to funds gener-
ated on site? Incentives and rewards could be developed with the participation of museum staff, as could the setting and measurement of goals for
attendance, volunteers, maintenance, community participation, and related
programming. If there is no reward for personal initiative, innovation, or
achievement, museums often remain static, neither serving their con-
stituencies nor fulfilling the aspirations of their employees.

Generally this study found that the methodology used for viewers to
receive information about the objects on display consisted of printed explanatory cards or printed labels (usually stating only culture, date, and
size), but not necessarily on each piece. With few exceptions, there is little
didactic information on walls or in cases that describes objects to museum
viewers or puts them into context. However, often a catalog can be bought
in Arabic, English, French, or Italian. This may reflect both the philosophy
and methodology of Jordanian museums, for often these museum exhibits
are meant to be interpreted by teachers and guides, not individually discovered or absorbed. Would the addition of comprehensive wall text, maps,
brochures, time lines, and extensive labeling encourage attendance? Possibly. But museums in the Middle East should not presume that all people are
literate. Are museums ignoring a portion of the adult population who might
come unannounced and cannot read? Perhaps another dimension for these
museums could be to address this issue and provide cultural and literacy
programs as components for new educational activities. Further, high-tech
computer and interactive displays, as well as audiotaped guided tours could
attract young audiences.

One of the issues important to Middle Eastern museums is whether
private museums should be allowed. There continues to be concern that allowing private museums might encourage illegal excavation or that they
might draw visitors (and thus revenue) away from the government museums. This implies that they would somehow be better. Both government
representatives and private collectors in Jordan have wrestled with this
issue. Several collectors spoke for their creation; many curators spoke
against their establishment. If this initiative is going to happen, laws need to
be changed. Before 1976 there were many collectors and dealers in antiquities. At that time a law was passed declaring that all antiquities were the
property of the Jordanian government and those private collections that existed were to be documented. Collectors were allowed to keep their objects

but were encouraged to donate them. The government purchased one private collection; other owners sought a private museum for their collections. The issue is still under discussion.

The decade of the 1980s in Jordan was the most productive period for museum development, with thirteen new museums and art centers opening during that time. What accounts for this flourish of activity? The internal dynamics of a society reaching critical mass, then this critical mass of people becoming educated and traveling abroad? The influx of new money, people, and sophistication from people fleeing war-torn Beirut, then later Kuwait and the Gulf? The changes in the legal system in Jordan? The oil boom in the Gulf? The way might have been made easier by these events, but in my opinion what made it happen was the fortuitous dynamism, dedication, and hard work of a few women.

All of the women in my study who are still living held university degrees. Many held a bachelor of arts degree in archeology from the University of Jordan, and several held higher degrees in that field. Others held degrees in law, art history, fine arts, education, geology, or political science. Four held doctorates. Their ages varied; some began their involvement with museums in the 1970s, however, the majority of women began later and were in their thirties. Although I was only concerned with administrators and curators, I should mention that there were other women working in the museum environment as typists, secretaries, file clerks, and receptionists. A high percentage (71 percent) of the administrators and curators in my study were married.

Did the women I interviewed know about feminist or women's organizations in Jordan? Yes, they were aware. Did they support these organizations? Two-thirds of the respondents said yes, they did. Women in Amman were more knowledgeable about feminist issues than those who lived in the smaller cities. Many of the women were sympathetic to feminist issues and felt they should be active, but were not (in Salt, Kerak, and Amman). Only two admitted to belonging to Jordanian women's organizations, however, some were members of the United Nations Women's Guild and the International Council of Museums (ICOM) through their job in the Department of Antiquities. The most common response to membership or involvement in women's empowerment organizations was that they had no time for such activities.

Women's organizations in Jordan exist on several levels for different purposes, mostly as support groups in the nonprofit sector. Their concerns have traditionally been politics and social welfare. Other international service organizations (such as Rotary) serve women in the business community. The professional women in my study had not developed or utilized such organizations fully as resources for mentoring, socializing, or networking.

To my question of why women had chosen museum work, an interest in archeology was the answer given most often. The responses that both men and women gave to the question indicated that museum work was an acceptable, protected, polite, and prestigious occupation for women to work in. Some women mentioned they were inspired by their parents who took them to museums as children, and most received support from their families to pursue higher education and careers in archeology; only a few were questioned or discouraged. Love of their work was a common response to my question of career choice. "You have to love your work—why else would you put up with the smell of this naphthalene!" said the curator of the Museum of Popular Traditions. "Museum work? It's a polite job," explained the curator of the Archeological Museum at the University of Jordan. Whether dealing with archeology, history, or contemporary art, dedication and a sense of doing something good for people, something that had meaning for the future, were most often the motives that made these women pursue their work. This is certainly the case in the founding of the Darat al Funun by the Abdul Hameed Shoman Foundation of the Arab Bank. There, a continuity of dedication to the arts began with the artist Fahrelnissa Zeid, who inspired Suha Shoman to create an arts center and pass on a legacy. In an interview, Shoman quoted the famous "Ask not what your country can do for you" line from President John F. Kennedy about service to one's country. She knew exactly what she and the foundation would like to do for Jordan, and she spoke of the analogy to the Medicis in Italy—who also were in the banking business.

To my question about discrimination, all the women in government museums answered in the negative. They said they felt none. Some were adamant that discrimination did not exist, although two admitted that in the past there might have been some preference for men who had just left military service. These women had modest aspirations: none volunteered that they wanted to become director of the Department of Antiquities. The former curator of the Jordan Archeological Museum despaired that a woman would ever achieve that post. Many desired further training in museology, which they acknowledged would put them in a position of consideration for advancement, but they felt they could not balance their work and their family life and continue their education.

Did I enjoy free communication with the women I interviewed? Yes and no; perhaps and maybe. Yes, we spoke the same languages, and if we did not, I had an interpreter. Yes, I received answers that came from the heart, evoked laughter, smiles, and even concern. But no, I also knew that answers were guarded. Perhaps they had done this before; they knew about personal investment. They knew I could come into their lives and then just leave; perhaps leave with a misquote in print. Being a woman helped me immensely. My rapport would have been difficult, at best, if I were a man. I had unquestioned access—alone—to women at many levels and in many places: museums, coffeehouses, homes, offices, and my apartment. Moreover, being a museum professional myself opened many doors and piqued curiosity. I often felt that people wanted to learn from me as much as I wanted to learn from them. But we did so in a dance of decorum, and we were always aware of that barrier between the visitor and the visited; the writer and the subject; the foreigner and the resident. Here was where my lack of formal training in anthropology became an issue, for as much as I wanted an objective analysis of the lives and work of the women I interviewed, I also wanted to share their lives—to become a friend, and establish a professional partnership. Does befriending negate critical observation? Distort analysis? Or did the relationships allow personal insights to be shared more readily? When I sought personal disclosure from these women, I realized I began participating in some of their lives and thus became part of their/our/my story.

It is sometimes easy to be seduced by the apparent impassiveness or tranquility with which many women operate in the Middle East. Does this suggest that they are unaware, naïve, resigned to their status, or that they see no need for change? Have they come to terms with their role in society? Are they afraid, personally and politically, to state their ideas, fears, needs, and hopes? I think not. Women have learned methods of communication that are nonthreatening to men.

Extrapolating to discussion about men, I learned that direct questioning was not always the most productive interview technique. I learned to ask the same questions in different ways. Many women were reticent to criticize or even discuss their relationships with their male coworkers. Four curators, from the Citadel, Salt, Irbid, and Jerash, admitted to a very good relationship; one in Salt described it as "in our official order: cooperating." Another woman working in a private art center/museum in Amman claimed "good equality." Yet later in response to a question about her biggest challenge, this same woman cited "acceptance by my co-workers [who were all male] as an equal." Was this ambivalence, honesty, or an example of ingrained doublespeak?

Jordan's museums are changing and growing. New directions and opportunities are being sought, new museums are being planned. Where are they headed? Will they be successful in attaining and maintaining an audience or able to change public attitudes and indifference? The first issue of *Arab Museum Newsletter, ICOM Arab* painted a broad canvas of needs and problems facing museums, including administrative autonomy, the creation of a training center for museology, stopping of illicit trade in antiquities, and repatriation of all cultural properties. Other issues that need to be addressed are financial assistance; the development of an active museum organization within the country; the need for contemporary ideologies; the need for better coordination between museums, schools, and universities; the upgrading of facilities; and the creation of complementary educational programs such as seminars and lectures (*Arab Museums Newsletter*, 2–3).

Several changes in the dynamics of Jordanian government and society bode well for museums. First, there has been a rededication to the cultural needs of the citizenry by the new government of King Abdullah II. In an article outlining new government policy, Prime Minister Abdur-Ra'uf S. Rawabdeh defined this new attitude toward the arts and culture: "As to culture, the government will give due attention to institutions that deal with cultural activities and we will halt the retreat in the role of arts" (*Jordan Times* 1999). Second, the Department of Antiquities has created the Directorate of Museums to deal with museum issues and development, and has chosen a woman as its first director.

This new climate for cultural development means that artifacts and documents from the past can be used as seeds for new growth, as the building blocks for the creation of an educated and enlightened society. Changes in the political dynamics of the Middle East can broaden the purpose of Jordan's museums to go beyond heritage and identity into present and future creativity.

During the 1990s Jordan began a process of political democratization and economic decentralization within the country. How has this affected museums? Have museums assumed a different role or benefited as a result of these policies? Indirectly, the answer would seem to be yes, given the attention being paid to development of museums as more tourist friendly and the discussion and planning of the economic revitalization anticipated around the site of the new National Museum—whether it be downtown or elsewhere in the city.

In achieving their full potential, museums need to take full advantage of the benefits of public spending on the arts, the economic benefits of employment, and the importance of cultural tourism. As the economy changes, deconstructing from being government-based toward privatization, businesses can find advantages in supporting cultural activities or creating new culturally based industries. This process has already begun. Examples can be found in the resurgence of interest in contemporary interpretation of crafts, in traditionally oriented interior design, and from the renovation of buildings such as the Abu Jaber stronghold in Yadoudah into the Kan Zaman restaurant and artist workshop complex for commercial, cultural, and artistic purposes.

Twenty-five years ago Jordanian museums suited the needs of the country. Today new museums are not only being dreamt of, they are being designed—for new audiences. But if change, support, resurgence of the arts, and establishment of new museums is to become reality, where is the new leadership? Where is the support? Jordan's minister of culture acknowledged in 1999: "There is a clear deficiency in supporting culture in our country, whether at the national or international level" (Al-Rfou'h 1999).

The establishment of museums in Jordan owes a great deal to the efforts of women. The women are needed now more than ever.

Afterword

My research reflects the history of the museums of Jordan up to the year 2000. Since that time there have been several changes. Two museums described in their development stage have opened, two others have been founded, and a fifth, championed by Queen Rania, progresses at breakneck speed.

The Numismatic Museum of the Jordan National Bank opened in 2002. The exhibit gallery is eight by twelve meters and contains twenty glass showcases each containing about one hundred sixty coins. Additionally, there are four perpendicular showcases where beads, bracelets, and other adornment are displayed. The library of the museum is one of the most comprehensive and specialized in the region. There is a lecture room on the upper floor of the bank building.

The National Museum, now called the City Hall Museum (the City Hall National Museum), was constructed in 2002 and is open to the public. It is located in downtown Amman at Ras al Ain. It bears little resemblance to the plans of the past.

The Arar Museum in Irbid announced itself with programs about the life and work of the poet Mustafa Wahbeh Tal (better known as Arar). The museum is located in the poet's home.

The Royal Car Museum, located in the new Al Hussein Park in Amman, opened in May 2002. More than sixty automobiles (dating from 1917) owned and driven by the late King Hussein are featured. The facility cost two million Jordanian dinars and covers an area of 5,200 square meters.

The Children's Museum, inspired by Queen Rania, is being built in Amman at the new Al Hussein Park complex at a cost of twenty-five million

93

Jordanian dinars. The complex includes landscaped gardens, children's playgrounds, and athletic fields. The museum is scheduled for mid-2003 completion and will target children aged ten and younger. It will provide educational presentations on the history and geography of Jordan.

Other museums mentioned under development remain in that state.

Appendixes

References

Index

Museums in Jordan

The Hashemite Kingdom of Jordan, located in the northwest corner of the Arabian Peninsula, is surrounded on the north by Syria, on the west by Israel and Palestine, to the east by Iraq, and to the south by Saudi Arabia. The overall area is approximately 35,000 square miles.

This strategic area between Asia, Africa, and Europe served as a crossroads for civilization even before the Persian, Greek, Roman, and Arab empires arrived, and humankind traveled across its historic trade routes. Jordan is heir to a continuum of human development and a continuity of historical occupation since Neolithic times. It is this background of diverse peoples and their monuments and artifacts that has nourished the character and content of Jordan's present-day museums.

The museums of Jordan reflect the influx of various peoples and cultures as empires advanced and receded over the area. In historical times, these migrations included Semitic peoples from Central Arabia, Assyrians, Persians, Egyptians, Arabs, Greeks, Romans, Mongols, and Turks. Around 1878, groups of Kurds, Armenians, and Circassians arrived in the area. The number of people from the Caucasus who immigrated to the Ottoman Empire was estimated at half a million; most of them were Circassians, a minority were Daghistani and Chechen. The Turkish Empire settled many of them in western Anatolia and the others in "Greater Syria." Land was given to the Circassians in Jordan in the areas of Amman, Wadi Seer, Na'ur, Sweilih, Jerash, Zarqa, Ruseifeh, and Sukhnah. A small community of Turkomans and Bahais, who immigrated from Iran around 1910, live in the northern Jordan Valley on land bought in 1879 by Abdul Baha Abbas, leader of the Bahai faith. A small number of Druze live in north Jordan near the Syrian border.

Evidence of historical habitation abounds in the museums of Jordan—from the ruins of the Old Testament kingdoms of Edom, Ammon, and Moab, the Nabataean city of Petra, the cities built by the Greeks and Romans, the castles erected by the Crusaders, the battlegrounds where Muhammad defeated Byzantine armies, and the forts of the Ottoman Empire.

Politics, history, and museums are closely related in Jordan. The Ministry of

Tourism and Antiquities has established a museum in every major urban center of the country and at many archeological sites, the desert castles being a notable exception. These museums reflect the ancient culture of their locale, and are frequently housed in readapted historic buildings. The following is a short history of nine major cities where the museums discussed in chaper 4, "Twelve Case Studies," are located.

Amman is the Rabbath-Ammon of the ancient world, the City of the Waters and Philadelphia to the classical world. Amman's history goes back thousands of years, long before recorded history. It may have been settled as early as the seventeenth century B.C.E. The Bible mentions that King David took shelter in Amman; Alexander the Great captured Amman when he marched east; and the Romans included Amman as the southernmost city of the Decapolis, naming it Philadelphia.

The city declined until the 1880s, when the Ottoman government settled Circassian refugees there. In 1893, the total city population was one thousand; it grew to three thousand in 1903 when the Hijaz Railway reached the city. In 1909, the first municipality was established; at the end of the Ottoman era in 1918, Amman was only a few square kilometers in size with a population of about five thousand. Today, with a population of slightly more than two million inhabitants, it is the capital of Jordan and hosts fifteen museums.

Aqaba is located in southern Jordan on the Gulf of Aqaba, an extension of the Red Sea. Known as Ezion Geber in biblical times, the city has a long history as a port. It became prosperous in the ninth century B.C.E. under King Solomon, who built his ships there to profit from trade with Africa. In Roman times, it was a stop on the road between Damascus and Egypt. Excavations at Tell Maquss and Tell Al-Khalifa confirm early copper-smelting activities. Nearby is Ayla, a site from the early Islamic period dating from between the mid-seventh and the early twelfth centuries C.E. Today it is a commercial shipping center and a water resort known for its reefs and coral and marine life. A historic fort, an archeological museum, a history museum, and an aquarium are located in the city.

Irbid, an educational and industrial center, is located in the northwest, near the Syrian border. Archeological evidence shows Irbid has been inhabited since the Bronze Age. Scholars debate whether Irbid was the biblical site of Beit Arbil. In Roman times it was known as Arabella (also Arabaelah or Arbila). Both the Department of Antiquities and Yarmouk University maintain museums in the city.

Jerash, thirty miles north of Amman, is the site of the well-preserved remains of the Greco-Roman city of Gerasa. Probably founded by Semites, it became an official Hellenistic city in 300 B.C.E. The settlement developed after annexation to the Roman province of Syria in the year 63. One of the cities of the Decapolis, Gerasa was an important commercial center with well-preserved temples, theaters, and baths until earthquakes in 746 and 647 devastated it. Declining thereafter, it was rediscovered by the German traveler Ulrich J. Seetzen in 1806. A modern city has grown up near the ruins. For many years an international cultural festival has been held at the ancient site in July. Jerash hosts the oldest of Jordan's museums.

Kerak, south of Amman, is positioned on ancient caravan routes and was known in antiquity as Kir, Kir Moab, Kir Heres, and, in Roman times, Characmoba. The massive Kerak fortress is the most impregnable in a chain built by the Crusaders in 1143. Mu'tah, the village around present-day Kerak, is the site of early Muslim clashes with Byzantine forces. The two sites house museums containing antiquities from the area.

Madaba, known in antiquity as the Moabite town of Medeba, is approximately twenty miles south of Amman on the ancient King's Highway, a trade route that has been in use for three thousand years. Settlement began in the Middle Bronze Age. Under Roman rule it grew to be a provincial town; in the Byzantine era, it flourished as a center known for its churches and mosaics. In the year 747 the town was destroyed by an earthquake and almost abandoned until the early nineteenth century, when several thousand Christians from Kerak resettled there. For years, seven international archeological groups have come to excavate. It is renowned for the Byzantine mosaic map of the Holy Land in the Greek Orthodox Church of St. George. The Department of Antiquities maintains an old house and ethnographic and archeological museums.

Petra, a UNESCO World Heritage Site, located in the southwest of Jordan, was settled long before the arrival of the Nabataeans who at one time ruled the Arab world as far north as Damascus. Walled in by towering rocks and accessible only through a narrow cleft called the Siq, it was a major city on the caravan trade route from southern Arabia. In 106, the city fell to the Romans, who continued its settlement. The Nabataeans left remains of an urban culture with more than eight hundred monuments, public, religious, and sepulchral architecture, and uniquely designed pottery. Classical writer Strabo wrote that Petra had magnificent houses and gardens. It is famous for its faáades cut in the rock with monuments and temples to the gods Dushara and Allat. After the Crusader period, knowledge of Petra was lost for centuries until Johann Ludwig Burckhardt rediscovered it in 1812.

The Department of Antiquities maintains two museums within the ancient city. A third is at the Petra Forum Hotel complex in Wadi Musa that was developed in cooperation with the University of Florence and Brown University.

Salt, located a short distance northwest of Amman, was founded on an Iron Age site that in Byzantine times was known as Saltos Hieraticon. Possibly deriving its name from the Latin *saltus*, or wooded valley, it was a thriving city in 1187 when Amman was just a village. It was the seat of the Ottoman administration for Jordan, and King Abdullah I chose it as his first capital. The new Emirate of Transjordan was proclaimed formally from the city's main square in 1921. The city features un-

changed architecture from the late Ottoman period. The Department of Antiquities maintains a folklore and archeological museum there, and it is the home of the
Schoolbook Museum at Al-Balqa University. A new national heritage museum is
being planned in the city.

Umm Qais, known in ancient times as Gadara or Gadar, is located in the ex-
treme northwest area of Jordan. It appears in historical records shortly after con-
quest by Alexander the Great in 333. The Maccabaean leader Alexander Jannaeus
destroyed the city in 100 B.C.E. In 63 B.C.E., under Pompey, the Romans rebuilt it. It
was one of the cities of the Decapolis and capital of the Roman district of the
Gedarites. The site was rediscovered in 1806 by Seetzen, who identified it as ancient
Gadara. A city known for its poets and philosophers, it was compared to the Hellenistic world's major centers of classical art. During the Byzantine era, the city declined and earthquakes destroyed much of it. It became known as Umm Qais during
the Middle Ages. An Ottoman village was later built on part of the Roman city. The
Department of Antiquities has established a museum at the site.

In 1999, a Directorate of Museums was established within the Department of
Antiquities to better support museums, identify their needs, and develop their services. Fawwaz Khreyseh became director general of antiquities within the Department of Antiquities and as such was administrative director of all government
archeological, historical, and folkloric museums. The information that follows
includes the museums of Jordan up to 2000. Entrance fees reflect cost to non-
Jordanians.

The Archeology Museum, University of Jordan
Name of museum: The Archeology Museum
Address: University of Jordan, Amman
Telephone: (06) 535-5000 Ext. 3417
Fax: (06) 535-5522 or 535-5511
E-mail: —
Director or curator: Manal Awamleh
Type of museum: Archeological
Founded: 1962
Governance: University of Jordan
Hours: 8 A.M.–5 P.M. Sunday through Thursday; closed Friday and Saturday
Entrance fee: Free
Number of staff: 3

Founded in 1962 by the University of Jordan, the museum opened in its present
facility in 1986 and shares a common courtyard with the university's National Heritage Museum. The museum was designed to serve the public as a showcase of

Jordan's ancient heritage and to serve the educational needs of archeology students. In that capacity, its facilities include exhibition halls, research workshops, photographic and drafting rooms, and a conservation laboratory.

The collection contains a wide range of objects in many media including marble, pottery, glass, metal, plaster, stone, and mosaics gathered from several sources: the Department of Antiquities, the excavations carried out by the archeology department at the university, purchases, and donations. The grounds and large courtyard surrounding the museum contain sculpture, inscriptions, and stonework. Inside, most of the pottery bowls, lamps, figurines, coins, and glass objects were excavated in Jerash, Rujm al-Kursi, Magass, and Tell al-Mazar by the university. The chronological display begins with the Prehistoric Age and ends with the Byzantine and Islamic periods. Labels and wall material are in Arabic and English.

Darat al Funun
Name of museum: Darat al Funun
Address: P.O. Box 910406, Amman
Telephone: (06) 464-3251
Fax: (06) 464-3253
E-mail: darat-al-funun@nets.com.jo
Web site: www.daratalfunun.org
Director or curator: Ali Maher
Type of museum: Contemporary art center
Founded: 1993
Governance: Abdul Hameed Shoman Foundation, now Khalid Shoman
    Foundation, Board
Hours: Saturday–Wednesday 10 A.M.–7 P.M.; Thursday 10 A.M.–8 P.M.;
    closed Friday
Entrance fee: Free
Number of staff: 12

Founded in 1993 by Suha Shoman and the Abdul Hameed Shoman Foundation of the Arab Bank, the Darat al Funun is located on Jebel Weibde in a complex of three buildings built in the 1920s on a hill alongside the remains of a sixth-century Byzantine church that had been constructed over an earlier Roman temple. It operates as a home for art and artists—a place free to the public, with exhibitions, a research library, studios and workshops, lecture and film presentations, and performing arts programs. The center presents eight exhibitions with thematically related performing arts programs, lectures, and films, and publishes catalogs. Many programs are presented in English; signage is in Arabic and English. There is an extensive art reference library above the galleries. Most of the books are in English, some in Arabic.

In the research study room, there is a small permanent display of antiquities found during the 1993 excavations of the property.

The upper building, the "Blue House," contains two galleries and offices. There is a small café outside. Steep stairways lead down the hill through the gardens to the main gallery and library. There are three exhibit halls inside. Beyond this building there is a sculpture courtyard and workshop and, further down the hill, the ancient church and temple platform area that is used for performing arts events.

Folklore Museum
Name of museum: Folklore Museum
Address: Ministry of Antiquities, P.O. Box 88, Amman
Telephone: (06) 465-1742
Fax: (06) 461-5848
E-mail: —
Director or curator: Eman al-Qudah
Type of museum: Ethnographic, folkloric
Founded: 1975
Governance: Department of Antiquities
Hours: 8 A.M.–5 P.M. daily
Entrance fee: One Jordanian dinar
Number of staff: 14

The museum is housed in the rooms to the right of and inside the entrance to the Roman Theater in downtown Amman.

The space mirrors that of the Museum of Popular Traditions on the opposite side of the theater entrance. Presentation in the five galleries focuses on the three areas of Jordanian culture: the desert, with examples of rugs, tents, equestrian items, tools, and weapons; the village, with installations on food preparation, basketry, wool processing, glassmaking, weaving, and women's costumes; and the towns and cities, with musical instruments, imported and inlaid furniture, carpets, and embroidery displayed in a recreated salon of the early twentieth century. The exhibits do not change. Also on view are displays of jewelry and pottery.

There is little wall text, identification, or explanation.

Geological Museum
Name of museum: Geological Museum
Address: P.O. Box 7, Amman
Telephone: (06) 585-7600
Fax: (06) 581-1866

E-mail: nra@nra.gov.jo
Director or curator: Suhair Shadid; Asma Zu'bi
Type of museum: Geology, energy, natural resources
Founded: 1989
Governance: Natural Resources Authority
Hours: 7:30 A.M.–2:30 P.M. Sunday through Thursday; closed Friday and Saturday
Entrance fee: Free
Number of staff: 3

The museum is located in Amman at the Eighth Circle in a building within the Natural Resources Authority complex. There are seven halls in the museum: Reception, Industrial, Rocks and Minerals, Oil and Gas Exploration, Story of the Earth, Ecology and Our Life, and Geological Mapping. These halls contain information, objects, and dioramas on the geological makeup of Jordan.

The displays are labeled in Arabic and English, and dioramas, posters, charts, and maps add to the learning experience. The sample collections contain approximately four hundred geological specimens indigenous to Jordan.

The purpose of the museum is to tell visitors about geology in general and specifically about the geology of Jordan. The museum lends from its collections and is active in educational seminars and conferences throughout the country.

The museum is considered an applied and informative institution that shows the different activities of the Natural Resources Authority.

Irbid Archeological Museum (New)
Name of museum: Irbid Archeological Museum
Address: P.O. Box 62, Irbid
Telephone: (02) 727-7066
Fax: (02) 724-1744
E-mail: —
Director or curator: Alia Khasowne
Type of museum: Archeological
Founded: 1966 (old), 1999 (new)
Governance: Department of Antiquities
Hours: By appointment
Entrance fee: Free
Number of staff: 5

The new museum, under construction, is a former Turkish prison located on Tell Irbid. This Ottoman serey is one of the oldest structures standing in Irbid. The walled compound contains exhibition space for archeological and folkloric objects in the restored offices, vaulted prisoner pens, and stables. Another section, with its own private entrance, will contain an archeological library and laboratories. The large central courtyard will be used for lectures and concerts. The offices of the Irbid Antiquities Department will also be located at the site. The exhibitions will focus on objects from the Irbid district and northwestern Jordan, include all media, and encompass prehistory through the Islamic periods.

Irbid Archeological Museum (Old)

The first Irbid Museum was also located on Tell Irbid but was subsequently relocated in 1984 to a building in the city that was not designed for easy public access. Presently housed in the department's facility, the small museum can exhibit only a small portion of its large holdings. The collection contains objects from the Paleolithic through the Islamic periods and includes stonework, ceramics, glass, coins, jewelry, and mosaics. There is little signage in Arabic or English and no climate control. The galleries are lighted naturally and with fluorescent lights. Storage of the vast collection of approximately five thousand pieces is in the basement.

Jerash Archeological Museum

Name of museum: Jerash Archeological Museum

Address: P.O. Box 12, Jerash

Telephone: (02) 635-2267

Fax: —

E-mail: —

Director or curator: Eman Oweis

Type of museum: Archeological

Founded: 1923

Governance: Department of Antiquities

Hours: 8 A.M.–6 P.M. daily

Entrance fee: Free; five dinars for entrance to the site

Number of staff: 6

Jerash boasts the oldest museum in Jordan. This small facility was established in 1923 under the Directorate of the Jordan Department of Antiquities in the early days of the Emirate of Transjordan. It was located in one of the rooms in the Temple of Artemis. The present museum facility was opened in 1985 by the Department of Antiquities; initially it was built to accommodate department employees, then served as a rest house. The museum experience is included in the entrance fee to the entire ancient Roman site.

The collection of approximately half a million items encompasses material found in the Jerash area from the Neolithic, Chalcolithic, Iron Age, Hellenistic, Nabataean, Roman, Byzantine, Umayyad, and Mamluk periods. A curved platform displays larger stone sculpture and mosaics from ancient Jerash's eighteen churches. The main hall, with its chronological exhibit, includes objects of pottery, glass, marble, stone, bronze, mosaics, jewelry, and coins. The displays are labeled in Arabic and English.

Jordan Archeological Museum
Name of museum: Jordan Archeological Museum
Address: Citadel Hill, P.O. Box 88, Amman
Telephone: (06) 463-8795
Fax: —
E-mail: —
Director or curator: Ahmad Ajajj
Type of museum: Archeological
Founded: 1951
Governance: Department of Antiquities
Hours: 8 A.M.–5 P.M. daily
Entrance fee: Two dinars
Number of staff: 20

Founded in 1951 by the Department of Antiquities under the British director G. Lankester Harding, the museum is located on the Citadel, at the top of a hill called Jabal al-Qala'a, overlooking downtown Amman. On the site are the ruins of a Roman temple.

The museum houses artifacts from all archeological sites in the country and includes objects from the Paleolithic, Neolithic, Chalcolithic, Bronze Age, Iron Age, Hellenistic, Nabataean, Roman, Byzantine, Islamic, and contemporary periods. The collection is vast and comprehensive, and includes pottery, mosaics, glass, precious stones, metals, and stonework. Many objects are decorative, others utilitarian, including tools and coins; other items are for adornment, grooming, and ritual such as statuary, votives, and commemorative objects.

Wall panels explain the many objects and put them in geographical or chronological context. The wall text and labels are in Arabic and English.

Jordan National Gallery of Fine Arts
Name of museum: Jordan National Gallery of Fine Arts
Address: P.O. Box 9068, Amman
Telephone: (06) 463-0128

Fax: (06) 465-1119
E-mail: JNG@nol.com.jo
Director or curator: Wijdan Ali, Ph.D., president, Royal Society of Fine Arts,
     and director of curatorial affairs; Rasmi Hamzeh, administrator
Type of museum: Contemporary fine art
Founded: 1980
Governance: Royal Society of Fine Arts
Hours: 10 A.M.–1:30 P.M.; 3 P.M.–6 P.M.; closed Tuesday
Entrance fee: One dinar
Number of staff: 6

Founded in 1980, the gallery is located on Jebel Weibde in a renovated villa opposite a park. The museum is governed by the Royal Society of Fine Arts, a private non-governmental, nonprofit institution. The society is run by a board of trustees that makes policy and monitors policy execution. The museum is managed by an administrator appointed by the society. The museum collects, presents, and documents contemporary works of art from Arab countries and the Islamic world.

The gallery has an extensive reference library of approximately one thousand books; a major strength is its collection of contemporary exhibition catalogs. The gallery publishes catalogs and documents exhibits. All signage and descriptive labeling is in Arabic and English. There are approximately eight exhibits annually. Borrowed exhibits reflect the mission of the gallery: to present contemporary art from, and relating to, the Islamic world.

The gallery encourages links with schools; workshops and tours of the galleries are available.

Museum of Jordanian Heritage, Yarmouk University
Name of museum: Museum of Jordanian Heritage
Address: Institute of Archeology and Anthropology, Yarmouk University, Irbid
Telephone: (02) 727-7276
Fax: —
E-mail: —
Director or curator: Mohammad Hatamleh
Type of museum: Anthropological and archeological
Founded: 1988 opened
Governance: Yarmouk University, Institute of Archeology and Anthropology
Hours: University hours; 8 A.M.–5 P.M. Sunday through Thursday; closed Friday
     and Saturday
Entrance fee: Free
Number of staff: 6

A courtyard outside the museum displays sarcophagi, carved stonework, and mosaics. The exhibits present a sequence of historical eras and cultural activities of all periods of Jordanian history from prehistory through the Bronze and Iron Ages, the Roman, Byzantine, Islamic, Ottoman periods to contemporary times.

Collections include pottery, glass, weavings, coins, utilitarian objects, costume, tools, implements, and jewelry. The mezzanine contains displays of Jordan's technology in the areas of mining, weaving, and glassmaking as well as collections of coins and amulets. An inner courtyard features the reconstruction of a north Jordanian village house. There is extensive signage in Arabic and English.

Museum of Popular Traditions
Name of museum: Museum of Popular Traditions
Address: Department of Antiquities, P.O. Box 88, Amman
Telephone: (06) 465-1760
Fax: —
E-mail: —
Director or curator: Huda Kilani
Type of museum: Folkloric, archeological
Founded: 1971
Governance: Department of Antiquities
Hours: 8 A.M.–5 P.M. daily
Entrance fee: One dinar
Number of staff: 5

The museum was founded in 1971 by Sa'adieh Al Tel and is located in downtown Amman in the rooms to the left inside the entrance of the Roman Theater. Originally conceived in 1966 for Jerusalem, it was moved to Jordan after the 1967 war with Israel. As with the Folklore Museum on the opposite side of the theater, the space was formerly used as offices by the Department of Antiquities.

The museum owns approximately twenty-three hundred objects including costumes, jewelry, cosmetic items, weavings, utensils, baskets, headdresses, and amulets. Specific focus in the five halls is on traditional women's costumes of both the East and West Banks. A lower hall contains Byzantine church mosaics from Jerash and Madaba that are on loan.

Displays are described in Arabic and English; wall text also includes original photographs.

Numismatic Museum, Central Bank of Jordan
Name of museum: Numismatic Museum, Central Bank of Jordan
Address: P.O. Box 37, Amman

Telephone: (06) 463-0301
Fax: (06) 463-8889
E-mail: —
Director or curator: Zahida Safer, Ph.D.
Type of museum: Numismatic
Founded: 1988
Governance: Central Bank of Jordan
Hours: By appointment
Entrance fee: Free
Number of staff: 3

Located in the business district of Amman on the mezzanine of the bank, the museum has its own side entrance and orientation room for scheduled groups.

The chronological display in the main gallery begins to the visitor's left. The collection of 2,385 coins is representative of those circulated in Jordan since the fourth century B.C.E. and includes examples of Nabataean, Greek, Roman, Byzantine, Islamic, Ottoman, Palestinian, and, after 1949, Hashemite Jordanian coins. Also on exhibit are commemorative coins struck for special occasions and paper money. Cases are low for easy viewing by children. The coins within each case are numbered and labeled in Arabic and English. On the walls, large graphics depict the history of coinage.

The museum borrows and lends coins. It is museum policy to collect two of each known issue.

Salt Folklore Museum
Name of museum: Salt Folklore Museum
Address: P.O. Box 85, Salt
Telephone: (05) 355-5651
Fax: —
E-mail: —
Director or curator: Muasar Audeh Hadidi, curator
Type of museum: Folklore
Founded: 1987
Governance: Department of Antiquities
Hours: 8 A.M.–5 P.M. daily
Entrance fee: Free
Number of staff: 7

Previously located with the Archeology Museum in the Salt Cultural Center, established by the Salt Development Corporation in 1987, the museum relocated to the second floor of a restored villa in 1997. The villa, built around 1892, had been used recently as a school. Accessed by a steep, narrow stairway, there are currently two rooms open with exhibits, as well as an outside patio.

The two small indoor exhibits document village and Bedouin society, using mannequins in costume to demonstrate food preparation and weaving along with the utilitarian objects and furniture typical in work and home settings. On the walls are examples of tools, musical instruments, and weapons from the area.

Jordanian Women and Museums

Positions and Institutions of Respondents

Name	Position/Title	Institution
Hidea Abaza	Founder, curator	Folklore Museum
Ruba Abu Dalu	Director, curator	Irbid Archeological Museum
HRH Wijdan Ali	President, Royal Society of Fine Arts	Jordan National Gallery
Khairieh Amr	Director, Directorate of Museums	Department of Antiquities
Naeimeh Asfour	Founder	Stamp Museum
Manal Awamleh	Curator, Archeology/ Heritage Museums	University of Jordan
Siham Balqar	Curator, retired	Jordan Archeological Museum (JAM)
Nuha Batchone	Director	The Gallery
Tamara Bermamet	Curator	JAM
Nazmieh Rida Tawfiq Darwish	Administrator	Department of Antiquities
Sawsan Al-Fakhri	Inspector of Antiquities	Aqaba District
Hanan Gammoh	Manager	Haya Cultural Center
Ghada Gordlow	Assistant	Central Bank Numismatic Museum
Muasar Audeh Hadidi	Curator	Salt Folklore Museum
Raida al-Haliq	Accountant, guide	Salt Folklore Museum
Lubna Hashem	Museum with No Frontiers	Ministry of Culture
Hyat al-Kadi	Curator	JAM

Widad Kawar	Collector, author	—
Alia Khasowne	Curator	Irbid Archeological Museum
Huda Kilani	Curator	Museum of Popular Traditions
Samia Khury	Curator	Jerash Archeological Museum
Hanan Al-Kurdi	Curator, administrator	—
Wafa'a Mansour	Administrator	The Museums at Madaba
Arwa Masaadeh	Curator	Kerak Museum
Jane Mufti	Executive administrator	Darat al Funun
Aida Naghawi	Curator, founder	Department of Antiquities
Hind Nasser	Activist, patron	—
Eman Oweis	Curator	Jerash Archeological Museum
Rabiha Qorani	Assistant	Central Bank Numismatic Museum
Rula Qsoos	Awareness Section	Department of Antiquities
Wafa' Qsouss	Administrator	Ministry of Culture
Eman al-Qudah	Curator	Folklore Museum
Zahida Safer	Curator	Central Bank Numismatic Museum
Nihad al Shabar	Curator	Yarmouk University
Suhair Shadid	Administrator	Geological Museum
Seteney Shami	Founder, former curator	Yarmouk University
Suha Shoman	Founder	Darat al Funun
Sa'adieh Al Tel	Founder, director	Museum of Popular Traditions
Norma Yessayan	Assistant	Jordan National Gallery
Muna Zaglow	Assistant	Museum of Popular Traditions
Samia Zaru	Educator, artist, activist	—
Princess Fahrelnissa Zeid	Artist, arts educator	Royal Art Institute of Fahrelnissa Zeid

Responses to Questionnaire

The author administered the following questionnaire to twenty-four women active in Jordan's museums between 1998 and 1999

Question: Should private museums be allowed in Jordan?
Responses: Yes: 7   No: 3   No opinion: 14
Comments:
Yes: Only for handicrafts; the government should get part of the admission fees.
No: Not at this stage; the market is too crowded; don't think the government will
      allow it, will compete.
Other: Contemporary museums would be all right; the government should buy
      their collections.

Question: Do you belong to any women's or feminist organizations?
Responses: Yes: 2   No: 6   No opinion: 14   Considered it: 2

Question: Do you support the feminist movement in Jordan?
Responses: Yes: 10   No: 3   No opinion: 9   Considered it: 2

Breakdown of Respondents by Age Groups

Respondents: Forty-two women comprising past and present curators, administrators, patrons, and founders, including twenty-four women active in museum work
between 1998 and 1999.

	Age Ranges of Respondents in Years				
No. of Women	20–30	30–40	40–50	50–60	61 and over
Active 1998–1999	4	11	5	4	0
Total	4	14	7	11	6

Types of Visual and Performing Arts Activities
at Forty-two Government and Private Museums

Classes: 9
Dance: 3
Exhibits: 35
Lectures: 15
Music: 5
Poetry: 1
Theater: 2
Total Number of Institutions: 42

Profiles of Twenty-four Jordanian Women
Actively Working in Museums

Married: 17
Unmarried: 7
Muslim: 18
Christian: 6
Circassian: 3
Palestinian: 4
Wearing *hijab*: 3
Educational Level:
    B.A. Degree: 17
    Graduate Degree: 6
    Other Degree: 1
    No Degree: 0

Museums and Art Centers in Major Cities of the Levant

Iraq

Abbasid Palace Museum, Baghdad
Arab Bath Socialist Party Museum, Baghdad
Aragouf Museum, Baghdad
Babylon Museum, Babylon
Baghdad Museum, Bab-al-Shargi, Baghdad
Basrah Museum, Basra
College of Arts Museum, Baghdad
The Iraqi Museum, Baghdad
Iraq Military Museum, Baghdad
Iraq Natural History Research Centre and Museum, Baghdad
Museum of Arab Antiquities, Baghdad
Museum of Iraqi Art Pioneers, Baghdad
Mustansiriya School Museum, Baghdad
National Museum of Modern Art, Baghdad
Natural History Museum, Mosul
Nirgal Gate Museum, Mosul
Popular Costume and Folklore Museum, Baghdad
Al-Ramadi Museum, Baghdad
Wasatani Gate Museum, Baghdad

Jordan

Ajlun Castle Museum, Ajlun
Al al Bayt University Museum, Mafraq
Aqaba Archeological Museum, Aqaba
Aquarium and Marine Station, Aqaba
Archeology Museum, Amman
Darat Al Funan, Amman
Folklore Museum, Amman
Fuheis Orthodox Museum, Fuheis
Geological Museum, Amman
Haya Cultural Center, Museum of Science, Amman
Irbid Archeological Museum, Irbid
Islamic Museum, Amman
Jerash Archeological Museum, Jerash
Jordan Archeological Museum, Amman
Jordan National Bank Numismatic Museum, Amman
Jordan National Gallery of Fine Arts, Amman
Kerak Archeological Museum, Kerak
King Abdullah Museum, Ma'an
Madaba Archeological Museum, Madaba
Madaba Folklore Museum, Madaba
Mafraq Archeological Museum, Mafraq
Martyr's Memorial Museum, Amman
Al-Mazar Museum, Mazar
Museum of Jordanian Heritage, Amman
Museum of Jordanian Postage, Amman
Museum of Popular Traditions, Amman
Museum of Sharif Hussein Bin Ali, Aqaba
Mu'tah University Museum, Mu'tah
National Heritage Museum, Amman
Numismatic Museum, Central Bank, Amman
Petra Archeological Museum, Petra
Petra Forum Museum, Wadi Musa
Petra Nabataean Museum, Petra
Salt Archeological Museum, Salt
Salt Folklore Museum, Salt
Schoolbook Museum, Salt
Sharif Hussein Bin Ali Museum, Amman
Umm Qais Archeological Museum, Umm Qais

Lebanon

Archeology Museum, American University of Beirut, Beirut
Daheshite Museum and Library, Beirut
Musée des Beaux Arts, Beirut
Musée Khalil Gibran, Besharre
Musée National, Beirut

Palestine, the West Bank, and Jerusalem

Al Qasabah, Nablus
Armenian Museum, Jerusalem
Artas Folklore Museum, Artas
Benshoof Museum, Jerusalem
Bethlehem Folklore Museum, Women's Union, Bethlehem
Birzeit University Fine Arts Gallery, Birzeit
Dar El Tifl El Arabi, Palestine Arab Folklore Center, Jerusalem
Ethnographic and Archeological Museums, Birzeit University, Birzeit
Franciscan Biblical Museum, Jerusalem
Gerizim Museum and Center, Nablus
Greek Orthodox Patriarchate Museum, Jerusalem
Hebron Museum, Hebron
Islamic Museum, Al-Aqsa Mosque, Jerusalem
Khalil Sakakini Cultural Centre, Ramallah
Museum of Contemporary Art, Bethlehem
Museum With No Frontiers, Ramallah
Palestine Archeological Museum (Rockefeller Museum), Jerusalem
Palestinian Folkloric Museum, In'ash El-Usra, El Bireh
Palestinian Center for Embroidery, Palestinian Heritage Center, Bethlehem
Ramallah Museum, Ramallah
Turathuna Centre for Palestinian Heritage, Bethlehem University, Bethlehem

Gaza

Arts and Crafts Village, Gaza City
Palestine Red Crescent Society Museums, Khan Younis and Gaza City
UNRWA Museum, Gaza City

Syria

Aleppo National Museum, Aleppo
Adnan Malki Museum, Damascus
Aleppo Castle Museum, Aleppo
Damascus Military Museum, Damascus
Department of Antiquities and Homs Museum, Homs
Hama Museum, Hama
Historical Museum of the City of Damascus, Damascus
Museum of Arabic Epigraphy, Damascus
National Museum of Damascus, Damascus
Popular Traditions Museum, Aleppo
Popular Traditions Museum, Damascus
Qasr Al Azm Museum, Damascus

Turkey

Archeology Museum, Istanbul
Asiyan Museum, Istanbul
Atatürk Museum, Istanbul
Ayasofya Museum, Istanbul
Calligraphy Museum, Istanbul
Carpet and Rug Museum, Istanbul
Istanbul Hisarlar Museum, Istanbul
Istanbul Museum of Painting and Sculpture, Istanbul
Kariye Museum, Istanbul
Mosaic Museum, Istanbul
Museum of Turkish and Islamic Art, Istanbul
Naval Museum, Istanbul
Rahmi Koç Industry Museum, Istanbul
Sadberk Hanim Museum, Istanbul
St. Irene Museum, Istanbul
Topkapi Palace Museum, Istanbul

Museology Course Syllabus

The following describes the components of Museology 1703, a single-semester course of sixteen weeks taught at the University of Jordan in 1999 by Nabil Khairy. The grading of the course was based on two written exams (25 percent and 40 percent of the course grade respectively), a paper (25 percent), and a practical show (10 percent).

General

The flow of the visitors in museums
Galleries, halls, entrances, doors, windows, floors, ceilings, walls, niches
Historical background of museums from ancient times to the present period
Identification of the terms *matahif* and *museology*
The main stages of museum development
The museum and communities
The museum and visitors
Museums and governmental institutions
Museums and media—newspapers, publications, TV, and broadcasting
Museums and private institutions
Plans and designs of the different types of museums
The role and function of the different types of museums

Service Units

Labs, administration units, cloakroom, bookshop, restaurant, publication center, public administration unit . . . parking lots for official employees, computer facilities, security

Collections

Methods of storing objects, climate in museums, monitoring climate, air pollution, harmful lighting levels, vibration, lack of precaution, lack of maintenance, shortage of energy

The Administration

Director, curators, laboratory technicians, research units, librarians, guards, security, finance office, publication staff, public relations

The Acquisition of Objects

Excavations, purchases, donations

Exhibitions

Permanent, contemporary, and traveling exhibitions; conferences on teaching materials

Showcases

Different types of showcases, free-standing objects, statues

Lighting, ventilation, and humidity

Different types, controls

References

Abranches, Henrique. 1983. *Proceedings of the Thirteenth General Conference, International Council of Museums [hereafter ICOM] 83*, 19–31. The Netherlands: ICOM.

Abu Dalu, Ruba. 1998a. Interview by author. Irbid, Jordan, Dec. 12.

———. 1998b. Questionnaire administered by author. Irbid, Jordan, Dec. 12.

Abu-Lughod, Ibrahim. 1999. Interview by author. Ramallah, West Bank, Feb. 24.

Abu-Lughod, Lila. 1986. *Veiled Sentiments: Honor and Poetry in a Bedouin Society.* Berkeley: Univ. of California Press.

Abu Nasr, Julinda, Nabil F. Khoury, and Henry T. Azzam, eds. 1985. *Women, Employment, and Development in the Arab World.* New York: Mouton Publishers.

Afkhami, Mahnaz, ed. 1995. *Faith and Freedom: Women's Human Rights in the Muslim World.* New York: Syracuse Univ. Press.

Ahmed, Jalal Uddin. 1984. "Wijdan Ali." *Arts and the Islamic World* 2, no. 1: 6.

Ajami, Jocelyn M. 1996. "Jordan's House of the Arts." *Aramco World Magazine*, July/Aug.: 2–7.

Albrecht, Lisa, and Rose M. Brewer, eds. 1990. *Bridges of Power: Women's Multicultural Alliances.* Philadelphia: New Society Publishers.

Ali, Wijdan. 1984. "The Collection of the Jordan National Gallery." *Arts and the Islamic World* 2, no. 1: 28–32.

———. 1998. Curriculum Vitae.

———. 1999. Interview by author. Amman, Jordan, March 31.

Ali, Wijdan, ed. 1990. *Contemporary Art from the Islamic World.* Northhampton, Mass.: Interlink.

———. 1996. "A Human-Scale Museum in Jordan." *Arts and the Islamic World* 4, no. 1: 9–11.

Amawi, Abla. 1996. "Women's Education in Jordan." In *Arab Women: Between Defiance and Constraint*, edited by Suha Sabbagh. New York: Olive Branch Press.

Al Ameri, Mohammad, ed. n.d. "Fakrh Al Nisa Zeid." Gallery brochure. Amman: Ministry of Culture.

Ames, Michael. 1986. *Museums, the Public, and Anthropology.* Vancouver: Univ. of British Columbia Press.

Amin, Qasim. 1899. *Tahrir al-mar'a* (The emancipation of women). Cairo.

"Amman 2010: City of Today with Roots in History." n.d. Amman: ROM Cultural Innovations.

Arab Museums Newsletter, ICOM Arab. 1995. Paris: ICOM.

Archabal, Nina. 1998. "Museums and Sustainable Communities." *Museum News* 77, no. 5: 31–35.

Ashrawi, Hanan. 1996. *This Side of Peace: A Personal Account.* New York: Touchstone Books.

El Assad, Junanah. 1990. *The National Heritage Museum: The University of Jordan.* Amman: Univ. of Jordan Press.

Atyyat, Taysir. 1998. Interview by author. Amman, Jordan, Dec. 30.

Atil, Esin. 1996. Interview by author. Washington, D.C.

Aviso (American Association of Museums, Washington, D.C.). 1999. Dec.

Awamleh, Manal. 1999. Interview by author. Amman, Jordan, March 14.

Ayed, Hasan. 1996. *This Is Jordan.* Amman: Adustour Commerce Press.

Badran, Margot. 1985. "Islam, Patriarchy, and Feminism in the Middle East." *Trends in History* 4, no. 1: 49–71.

Balqar, Siham. 1999. Interview by author. Amman, Jordan, April 12.

Balqar, Siham, and Musa Mustapha Zayyat. 1994. "The Jordan Archeological Museum, Amman; Exhibiting a Permanent Collection." In *Encounter "Museums, Civilization, and Development" (1994: Amman, Jordan),* 26–30 April 1994, 155–57. Paris: ICOM.

Barakat, Halim. 1993. *The Arab World: Society, Culture, and State.* Berkeley: Univ. of California Press.

Basson. 1984. "Male Emigration and the Authority Structure of Families in Northwest Jordan." In *JWSAW.* Beirut: Beirut Univ. College.

Bell, Gertrude, ed. 1927. *The Letters of Gertrude Bell.* London: Ernest Benn.

Bermamet, Tamara. 1998. Interview by author. Amman, Jordan, Dec. 30.

———. 1999. Interview by author. Amman, Jordan, April 12.

Bienkowski, Piotr, ed. 1991. *Treasures from an Ancient Land: The Art of Jordan.* [Liverpool] UK: National Museums and Galleries on Merseyside.

Bikai, Pierre M., May Sha'er, and Brian Fitzgerald. n.d. *The Byzantine Church at Darat al Funun.* Amman: Abdul Hameed Shoman Foundation.

Bisharat, Suhail. 1984. "Art Today in Jordan." *Arts and the Islamic World* 2, no. 1: 33–35.

———. 1991. "Amman Newsletter." *Arts and the Islamic World* 91, no. 20: 72.

———. 1994. "The Role of Collections, Exchanges in Museum Cultural Policy." In *Museums, Civilization and Development.* Paris: ICOM.

Bisheh, Ghazi. 1998. Interview by author. Amman, Jordan, Nov. 21.

Bouran, Alia Hatough. 1999. Interview by author. Amman, Jordan, Apr. 5.

Brand, Laurie A. 1998. *Women, the State, and Political Liberalization: Middle Eastern and North African Experiences.* New York: Columbia Univ. Press.

Broshi, Magen. 1994. "Archeological Museums in Israel: Reflections on Problems of National Identity." In *Museums and the Making of "Ourselves": The Role of Objects in National Identity.* New York: Leicester Univ. Press.

Brown, Claudine. 1994. Foreword to *Gender Perspectives: Essays on Women in Museums,* edited by Jane R. Glaser and Artemis A. Zenetou, xiii–xvi. Washington, D.C.: Smithsonian Institution Press.

Chatty, Dawn. 2000. "Women Working in Oman: Individual Choice and Cultural Constraints." *International Journal of Middle East Studies* 32, no. 2: 241–54.

Conkey, Margaret W., with Sarah H. Williams. 1991. "Original Narratives: The Political Economy of Gender in Archeology." In *Gender at the Crossroads of Knowledge: Feminist Anthropology in the Postmodern Era,* edited by Micaela di Leonardo. Berkeley: Univ. of California Press.

Crespo, Hernan. 1989. "New Forms of Presentation." *Museums, Generators of Culture, ICOM 89, Reports and Comment ICOM, Seventy-Fifth General Conference.* The Netherlands: ICOM.

Dana, John Cotton. 1917. *The New Museum.* Woodstock, Vt.: Elm Tree Press.

"Darat al Funun: The Function." 1994. Gallery sheet. Amman: Abdul Hameed Shoman Foundation.

Darat al Funun: Art, Architecture, Archeology. 1998. Amman: Abdul Hameed Shoman Foundation.

Darwish, Nazmieh Rida Tawfiq. 1984. "Um Qais." *Arts and the Islamic World* 2, no. 1: 64–77.

———. 1994. "School Visits to Archeological Museums in Jordan." In *Encounter "Museums, Civilization, and Development" (1994: Amman, Jordan),* 183–85. Paris: ICOM.

———. 1999. Interview by author. Kerak, Jordan, Apr. 6.

Davis, Terence G., ed. 1964. *A Short Guide to the Amman Museum.* Amman: The Friends of Archeology.

De Maio, Anca. March 1998. "Princess Wijdan Ali, Art and Diplomacy, Perfect Compatibility." http://star.arabia.com.

Department of Antiquities of Jordan. 1994. *Archaeological and Ethnographic Museums in Jordan.* Amman: Department of Antiquities.

Department of Antiquities of Jordan. 1994. *The Jordan Archeological Museum: A Brief Description.* Amman: Department of Antiquities.

Department of Publication of Jordan. 1979. *The Jordanian Woman.* Amman: Department of Publication.

Directory of Museums in the Arab Countries. 1995. Paris: ICOM.

Al-Fakhri, Sawsan. 1999a. Interview by author. Aqaba, Jordan, April 19.

———. 1999b. Questionnaire administered by author. Aqaba, Jordan, April 19.

"Feminist Movement Rewriting 'His Story.'" 1999. Aug. 8. http://star.arabia.com.

Fistere, Isobel, and John Fistere. n.d. *Jordan the Holy Land.* Beirut: Middle East Export Press.

Fitzgerald, Marilyn Hicks. 1973. *Museum Accreditation: Professional Standards.* Washington, D.C.: American Association of Museums.

Friedl, Erika. 1995. "Notes from the Village." In *Reconstructing Gender in the Middle East: Tradition, Identity, and Power,* edited by Fatma Müge Göçek and Shiva Balaghi. New York: Columbia Univ. Press.

Gallagher, Nancy. 1995. "Women's Human Rights on Trial in Jordan: The Triumph of Toujan al-Faisal." In *Faith and Freedom: Women's Human Rights in the Muslim World,* edited by Mahnaz Afkhami, 209–31. New York: Syracuse Univ. Press.

Gendzier, I. 1982. Foreword to *The Hidden Face of Eve: Women in the Arab World,* by Nawal Saadawi. Boston: Beacon Press.

Glaser, Jane R., and Artemis A. Zenetou, eds. 1994. *Gender Perspectives: Essays on Women in Museums.* Washington, D.C.: Smithsonian Institution Press.

Göçek, Fatma Müge, and Shiva Balaghi. 1995. *Reconstructing Gender in the Middle East: Tradition, Identity, and Power.* New York: Columbia Univ. Press.

Golvin, L. 1967. "Jordan: Setting up a Museum of Folkarts and Traditions." *UNESCO Report,* Ws/0367.67. CLT: Paris: UNESCO.

Goussous, Nayef G. 1998. *Origin and Development of Money.* Amman: Arab Bank.

———. 1999. Interview by author. Amman, Jordan, April 6.

Goussous, Nayef G., and Khalaf F. Tarawneh. n.d. *Coinage of the Ancient and Islamic World.* Amman: Arab Bank.

Graham-Brown, Sarah. 1988. *Images of Women: The Portrayal of Women in Photography of the Middle East, 1860–1950.* New York: Columbia Univ. Press.

Haddad, Yvonne Hazbek, and John L. Esposito, eds. 1998. *Islam, Gender, and Social Change.* New York: Oxford Univ. Press.

Hadeed, Nidal. 1998. Interview by author. Amman, Jordan, Dec. 15.

Hadidi, Muasar. 1999. Questionnaire administered by author. Salt, Jordan. Mar. 20.

Haghandoqa, Mohammad Kheir. 1985. *The Circassians.* Amman: Rafidi Print.

Al Haliq, Raida. 1999. Interview by author. Salt, Jordan, Mar. 20.

Hamdan, Dina. 2000. "Govt Accused of Shirking Responsibilities before U.N. High Commissioner for Human Rights." *Jordan Times.* May 11, 3.

Hamzeh, Rasmi. 1998. Interview by author. Amman, Jordan, Dec. 31.

Harding, G. Lankester. 1959. *The Antiquities of Jordan.* Amman: Butterworth Press.

Hardoy, Jorge E. 1986. "The Popular Sum of Knowledge and the Museum." Paris: ICOM.

Harik, Ramsey, and Elsa Marston. 1996. *Women in the Middle East: Tradition and Change.* Danbury, Conn.: Grolier Publishing.

Hashem, Lubna. 1999. Interview by author. Amman, Jordan, April 13.

Hatamleh, Mohammad. 1998a. Interview by author. Irbid, Jordan, Dec. 2.

———. 1998b. Questionnaire administered by author. Irbid, Jordan, Dec. 2.

Hijab, Nadia. 1988. *Womenpower: The Arab Debate on Women and Work.* Cambridge: Cambridge Univ. Press.

Hourani, Albert. 1991. *A History of the Arab Peoples.* Cambridge: Harvard Univ. Press.

Ibrahim, Moawiyah. 1988. Preface to *Museum of Jordanian Heritage.* Irbid: Al Kutba.

International Council of Museums (ICOM). *ICOM, Eleventh General Assembly of ICOM, ICOM Statutes.* 1974. Copenhagen: ICOM.

International Directory of Islamic Cultural Institutions. 1989. Istanbul: Research Centre for Islamic History, Art, and Culture.

Islamic Arts Foundation. 1982–83. "H.R.H. Princess Wijdan Ali of Jordan." *Arts and the Islamic World* 1, no. 1: 49–51.

Japan International Cooperation Agency (JICA). (1996?). *Final Report: The Study on the Tourism Development Plan in the Hashemite Kingdom of Jordan,* 4–46. Amman: Ministry of Tourism and Antiquities and JICA.

Department of Antiquities, Jordan. 1994. *The Jordan Archeological Museum: A Brief Description.* Amman: Department of Antiquities.

Jordan: Keys to the Kingdom. 1995. Amman: National Press.

Jordan Times. 1998–99. "Jordanian Society." Dec. 31 and Jan. 1, sec. 3.

———. 2000. "Queen Tours Jerash Governate." Jan. 26, sec 3.

———. 1999. "Rawabdeh Outlines Tough Agenda in Policy Statement," Apr. 4, sec. 3.

Kandiyoti, Deniz, ed. 1996. *Gendering the Middle East: Emerging Perspectives.* Syracuse, N.Y.: Syracuse Univ. Press.

Kaplan, Flora E. S., ed. 1994. *Museums and the Making of "Ourselves": The Role of Objects in National Identity.* Leicester: Leicester Univ. Press.

Karp, Ivan, Christine Mullen Kreamer, and Steven D. Lavine, eds. 1992. *The Politics of Public Culture.* Washington, D.C.: Smithsonian Institution Press.

Karp, Ivan, and Steven D. Lavine, eds. 1991. *Exhibiting Cultures: The Poetics and Politics of Museum Display.* Washington, D.C.: Smithsonian Institution Press.

Kawar, Widad. 1999. Interview by author. Amman, Jordan, April 17.

Keddie, Nikki R., and Lois Beck. 1979. "Problems in the Study of Middle Eastern Women." *International Journal of Middle East Studies* 10 (May): 225–40.

———, eds. 1991. *Women in Middle Eastern History: Shifting Boundaries in Sex and Gender.* New Haven: Yale Univ. Press.

Khairy, Nabil. 1998. "Archeology in Jordan: Future Perspective." *Campus News* (Univ. of Jordan), no. 100: 13.

———. 1999. Interview by author. Amman, Jordan, Mar. 17.

Al-Khalil, Samir. 1991. *The Monument: Art, Vulgarity, and Responsibility in Iraq.* London: Andre Deutsch.

Khouri, Rami. 1999. Interview by author. Amman, Jordan, Apr. 7.

Kilani, Huda. 1999a. Interview by author. Amman, Jordan, Mar. 2.

———. 1999b. Questionnaire administered by author. Amman, Jordan, Mar. 24.

Al-Kurdi, Hanan. 1999a. Interview by author. Amman, Jordan, Apr. 13.

———. 1999b. Questionnaire administered by author. Amman, Jordan, Apr. 13.

Layne, Linda. 1981. "Women in Jordan's Workforce." *MERIP Reports* 95: 19–23.

———. 1994. *Home and Homeland: The Dialogics of Tribal and National Identities in Jordan.* Princeton, N.J.: Princeton Univ. Press.

Lumley, Robert, ed. 1988. *The Museum Time Machine: Putting Cultures on Display.* London: Routledge/Comedia.

Maffi, Irene. 1999. "On the Usage of History by the State Power: The Museums and the Building of National Identity after 1967." *Jordanies*, no. 5–6: 84–99.

Maher, Ali. 1998. Interview by author. Amman, Jordan, Dec. 10.

Malt, Carol. 1999. "Darat al Funun: Celebrating the Tenth Anniversary Exhibition of Contemporary Arab Artists." *Jordan Times.* 1 Jan., sec. 3.

Markarian, Zohrab. 1986. *King and Country.* London: Hutchinson Benham.

Masaadeh, Arwa. 1999. Interview by author. Kerak, Jordan, Apr. 6.

Masry, Abdullah H. 1994. "Archeology and the Establishment of Museums in Saudi Arabia." In *Museums and the Making of "Ourselves": The Role of Objects in National Identity*, edited by Flora E. S. Kaplan, 125–67. Leicester: Leicester Univ. Press.

Mernissi, Fatima. 1987. *Beyond the Veil: Male-Female Dynamics in a Modern Muslim Society.* Bloomington: Indiana Univ. Press.

Mershen, Birgit. 1988. Introduction to *Museum of Jordanian Heritage*, Yarmouk University, 12–15. Irbid: Al Kutba.

Ministry of Culture of Jordan. 1999. "The Mission of the Ministry." Info@culture .gov.jo.

Ministry of Tourism and Antiquities of Jordan. 1996. *The Study of the Tourism Development Plan in the Hashemite Kingdom of Jordan.* Japan International Cooperation Agency (JICA). Amman: Ministry of Tourism and Antiquities.

———. n.d. "Working Paper on the National Museum of Jordan."

Mitri, George, ed. 1979. *Dictionary of the Arab Language.* Beirut.

Moghadam, Valentine. 1993. *Modernizing Women: Gender and Social Change in the Middle East.* Boulder, Colo.: Lynne Rienner.

———. 1998. *Women, Work, and Economic Reform in the Middle East and North Africa.* Boulder, Colo.: Lynne Rienner.

———, ed. 1994. *Gender and National Identity*. London: Zed Books.

———. 1996. *Patriarchy and Economic Development: Women's Positions at the End of the Twentieth Century*. New York: Clarendon Press.

Moors, Annelies, ed. 1995. *Discourse and Palestine: Power, Text, and Context*. Amsterdam: Het Spinhuis.

Mostyn, Trevor. 1981–82. "Jordan's National Gallery Looks East and West." *UR* (Iraqi Cultural Centre, London), no. 1: 79.

Mufti, Jane. 1999a. Interview by author. Amman, Jordan, Apr. 4.

———. 1999b. Questionnaire administered by author. Amman, Jordan, Apr. 4.

Mujahid, G.B.S. 1985. "Female Labor Force Participation in Jordan." In *Women, Employment, and Development in the Arab World*, edited by Julinda Abu Nasr, Nabil F. Khoury, and Henry T. Azzam. New York: Mouton Publishers.

Museum of Jordanian Heritage, Institute of Archeology and Anthropology. 1988. Amman: Al Kutba.

"Museums in Jordan." n.d. *Travel Jordan: A Tourist Factsheet*. Amman: Al Kutba and the Jordanian Ministry of Tourism.

Naghawi, Aida. 1999. Interview by author. Amman, Jordan, Jan. 27.

Naghawi, Aida, and Rula Qsoos. 2000. Interview by author. Amman, Jordan, Jan. 5.

Nashashibi, Salwa Mikdadi, et al. 1994. *Forces of Change: Artists of the Arab World*. Washington, D.C.: International Council for Women in the Arts and the National Museum of Women in the Arts.

Naser, Rabiha D. 1985. "Women in Leadership Positions and Decision Making." Paper presented at National Conference of Jordanian Women: Current Status and Future Prospects, organized by the General Union of Jordanian Women, Amman.

Nashat, Guity. 1995. Introduction to *Women in Islam*, by Wiebke Walther. Princeton, N.J.: Markus Weiner.

Nasser, Hind. 1999. Interview by author. Amman, Jordan, Mar. 17.

Noor al Hussein. 1991. Foreword to *Treasures from an Ancient Land: The Art of Jordan*, edited by Piotr Bienkowski, vii. [Liverpool] UK: National Museums and Galleries on Merseyside.

The Official Museum Directory. Washington D.C.: National Register Publishing Co.

Okita, Silas. 1997. "Museum Ethics." In *Museum Ethics*, edited by Gary Edson, 129–39. New York: Routledge.

Oweis, Eman. 1994. "Difficulties Arising from Present Structure of Our Museums." In *Encounter "Museums, Civilization, and Development" (1994: Amman, Jordan)*, 26–30 April 1994, 171–74. Paris: ICOM.

———. 1999a. Interview by author. Jerash, Jordan, Apr. 2.

———. 1999b. Questionnaire administered by author. Jerash, Jordan, Apr. 2.

Parinaud, André. 1984. *Fahr El Nissa Zeid*. Amman: Royal National Jordanian Institute Fahrelnissa Zeid of Fine Arts.

Pearce, Susan M. 1990. *Archaeology Curatorship*. Leicester: Leicester Univ. Press.

———. 1992. *Museums, Objects, and Collections*. Leicester: Leicester Univ. Press.

Pieterse, Jan Nederveen. 1995. "Aesthetics of Power: Time and Body Politics." In *Discourse and Palestine: Power, Text and Context*, edited by Annelies Moors. Amsterdam: Het Spinhuis.

Porterfield, Todd B. 1994. "Western Views of Oriental Women in Modern Painting and Photography." In *Forces of Change: Artists of the Arab World*, by Salwa Mikdadi Nashashibi et al., 58–71. Washington, D.C.: International Council for Women in the Arts and the National Museum of Women in the Arts.

Qsoos, Rula. 2000. Interview by author. Amman, Jordan, Jan. 15.

al-Qudah, Eman (Iyman El Qudah). 1994. "Folklore Museum." *ICOM 1994*, 165–66.

———. 1998. Interview by author. Amman, Jordan, Dec. 14.

———. 1999. Questionnaire administered by author. Amman, Jordan, Jan. 15.

Quinn, Naomi. 1977. "Anthropological Studies on Women's Status." *Annual Review of Anthropology* 6: 181–225.

Quteishat, Khadijeh. 1998. *Campus News* (Univ. of Jordan) 9.

Al-Rfou'h, Faisel. 1999. "Remarks on the Role of Culture in Sustainable Development." In *Culture Counts: Financing, Resources, and the Economics of Culture in Sustainable Development*. Washington, D.C.: World Bank and UNESCO.

Ramadan, Arslan Bakig. n.d. (1984?) *Amman Yesterday and Today*. London: W. S. Cowell.

Rishaidat, Mohamad Omar. 1994. "Museums, Roles, Development and Obstacles." In *Museums, Generators of Culture: Minutes of the 12th Annual Meeting, The Hague, 29 August–3 September 1989*, edited by Anton Korteweg, 175–82. Paris: ICOM.

"The Role of Museums and Museum Personnel." 1994. In *Museums, Civilization and Development*. Paris: ICOM.

Royal Society of Fine Arts. 1980. *Inaugural Brochure*. Amman.

Saadawi, Nawal. 1982. *The Hidden Face of Eve: Women in the Arab World*. Translated by Sharif Hetata. Boston: Beacon Press.

Sabbagh, Suha, ed. 1996. *Arab Women: Between Defiance and Constraint*. New York: Olive Branch Press.

Sadek, Mohammed-Moain. 1994. "Archeological Museums in Palestine: Reality and Prospectives." In *Museums, Civilization and Development*, 287–91. Paris: ICOM.

Safer, Zahida. 1998. Interview by author. Amman, Jordan, Dec. 3.

Said, Edward W. 1978. *Orientalism*. London: Rutledge.

Salim, Naza. 1977. *Iraq Contemporary Art*. Lausanne: Sartec.

Sayigh, Rosemary. 1996. "Researching Gender in a Palestinian Camp: Political, Theoretical and Methodological Issues." In *Gendering the Middle East: Emerging Perspectives*, edited by Deniz Kandiyoti. Syracuse, N.Y.: Syracuse Univ. Press.

Semseddin, Sami. 1880. *Kadinlar*. Istanbul.

Shaaban, Bouthaina. "Arab Women Novelists: Creativity and Rights." *Middle East Women's Studies Review* 14, no. 4: 1–6.

Al-Shabbar, Nihad, and Mujahed Al Muhaisen. 1994. "An Introduction to the Museum of Jordanian Heritage," 137–40. In *Museums, Civilization and Development*. Paris: ICOM.

Shadid, Suhair. 1999. Interview by author. Amman, Jordan, Apr. 3.

Shami, Seteney. 1999. Interview by author. Washington, D.C., U.S., Nov. 21.

Shami, Seteney, and Lucine Taminian. 1990. "Women's Participation in the Jordan Labour Force: A Comparison of Urban and Rural Patterns." In *Women in Arab Society: Work Patterns and Gender Relations in Egypt, Jordan, and Sudan*, by Seteney Shami et al. Providence, R.I.: Berg Publishers.

Shoman, Suha. 1999. Interview by author. Amman, Jordan, Jan. 26.

Shuraydeh, Hiyam, and Adel Lutfi. 1985. "Working Woman in Jordan: A Study and Analysis of Her Characteristics." Paper presented at National Conference of Jordanian Women: Current Status and Future Prospects, organized by the General Union of Jordanian Women, Amman.

Sims, James, and Patrick Rogan. 1997. *Jordan National Museum Conceptual Plan*. n. p.: Threshold Studio Plan.

Souan, K. C. R. n.d. *Philatelic History of Jordan. LXX 1920–1990*. El Incognitos Diamond Jubilee. Kuwait: K.D.R. Souan.

The Star. 1999. Jan. 14–17. Vol. 9, no. 32.

Stétié, Salah. 1982. "Some Thoughts on the Muslims and Their Monumental Heritage." Paper delivered at the Arts in Islamic Lands conference, Farnham Castle, England.

Strobel, M., and C. Odim, eds. 1988. *Restoring Women to History: Teaching Packets for Integrating Women's History into Courses on Africa, Asia, Latin America and the Caribbean, and the Middle East*. Bloomington, Ind.: Organization of American Historians.

Al-Tal, Nesreen. 1994. "A Museum for the Disabled." In *Museums, Civilization and Development*, 141–42. Paris: ICOM.

Talal, Basma bint. 1999. Jordanian National Forum for Women. Index. Arabia.com.

Ibn Talal, Hussein. [1965.] Foreword to *Jordan the Holy Land*, by Isobel Fistere and John Fistere. Beirut: Middle East Export Press.

Al Tel, Sa'adieh. n.d. Introduction to *Jordan Museum of Popular Traditions*. Amman: Jordan Press Foundation.

Tel, Waf'a. 1998. Interview by author. Amman, Jordan, Dec. 9.

Tucker, Judith E. 1988. "Women in the Middle East." In *Restoring Women to History: Teaching Packets for Integrating Women's History into Courses on Africa, Asia, Latin America and the Caribbean, and the Middle East*, edited by M. Strobel and C. Odim. Bloomington, Ind.: Organization of American Historians.

Tukan, Jafar. 1984. "Extension to the National Gallery." *Arts and the Islamic World* 2, no. 1: 45–47.

———. 1998. Interview by author. Amman, Jordan, Dec. 21.

Twal, Natasha. 1999. "Feminist Movement: Rewriting 'His Story.' " Aug. 8. http://star.arabia.com.

UNESCO. 1966. *UNESCO Statistical Yearbook*. Lanham, Md.: UNESCO Publishing and Bernan Press.

Uris, Leon. 1984. *The Haj*. New York: Doubleday.

Van Dijk, Hans. 1993. "Double Standards." *Dossier hond en Hamer*. The Netherlands: Grafisch Atelier Daghicht Endhoven.

Walther, Wiebke. 1995. *Women in Islam from Medieval to Modern Times*. Princeton, N.J.: Markus Weiner.

Warrick, Catherine. 1998. "Gender and the Politics of Culture in Jordan." Paper delivered at the Middle East Studies Association annual meeting, Chicago.

Weil, Stephen E. 1997. "Romance versus Realism: A Reflection on the Nature of Museums." *Museum News* 76, no. 2: 52–67.

Williams, B. F. 1990. "Nationalism, Traditionalism, and the Problem of Cultural Inauthenticity." In *Nationalist Ideologies and the Production of National Cultures*, edited by R. G. Fox. Washington, D.C.: American Anthropological Association.

The World Bank. *Cultural Heritage and Development: A Framework for Action in the Middle East and North Africa*. 2001. Washington D.C.: International Bank for Reconstruction and Development/World Bank.

Yegenoglu, Meyda. 1998. *Colonial Fantasies: Toward a Feminist Reading of Orientalism*. New York: Cambridge Univ. Press.

Yessayan, Norma. 1999. Interview by author. Amman, Jordan, Jan. 30.

Yuval-Davis, Nira. 1997. *Gender and Nation*. London: Sage Publications.

Zaru, Maha. 1996. "A Thesis Report Subject to the College of Architecture and Art." Master's thesis, Jordan Univ. for Women.

———. 1998. Interview by author. Amman, Jordan, Nov. 23.

Zaru, Samia. 1999. Interview by author. Amman, Jordan, Mar. 26.

Zayyaden, Fowzia. 1999. Interview by author. Kerak, Jordan, Apr. 6.

Zuhdi, Bashir. 1988. *Museums, Amman*. Amman: Ministry of Culture.

Index

129

United Women's Social Organization, 20
university collections, xxi, 44
University of Jordan, 5, 9, 27–28
urbanism, 4
Uris, Leon, xix
U'ruba School, xxxiii
USAID, 28, 64

Victory Arch (Baghdad), 38
village life, 53, 75, 85
visual and performing art activities, 112
volunteerism, 12–13, 66
voting rights, 10

waqf system, xiv, 27
wars, 11, 36
Weil, Stephen, 37
Werdan, Muhammed Ali, xxvii
West Bank, 114
Westerners, xvii, 6, 19
Widad Kawar Arab Heritage Collection of
   Palestinian and Arab Costumes, 80
women: advice of for those interested in
   museum work, 45–46; age of as
   museum workers, 13, 88, 112;
   attraction of museum work to, 40–43,
   89; communication of with interviewer,
   90; as curators, 26–27; as depicted on
   coins, 74; displays of articles made by,
   xiv, xxi, 49–50, 75; as driving force
   behind museums, xxv–xxvi, 88; dual
   role of, 10, 13–15; education of, 5–6,
   8–9; influence on messages of displays,
   39–40; influence on museums, xvi,
   110–11; interest in National Gallery,
   64; museums proposed by, xxiv; as

museum workers and collectors, 46,
   113; personal needs of as museum
   workers, 84; relationships of with men,
   90–91; representation of in Dead Sea
   Museum, xxvii; rights of, 10, 18–21;
   special touch for museums among,
   43–46; in workplace, 3–7, 9–18, 25–27
Women's Federation, 20
women's organizations, 12, 14, 18–20, 84,
   88–89
work, 3–5, 6–7, 9–18, 25–27
Working Paper on the National Museum, xxx

Yarmouk University, 9, 27, 28, 33, 111
Yassin, Khier, xxvi
Yessayan, Norma, 13, 111
Yuval-Davis, Nira, 6

Zaglow, Muna, 42, 72, 77, 111
Zaru, Samia: accomplishments of, 81; as
   artist/educator, 77, 111; Arts Week
   and, 62; development of educational
   program by, 30; on educational
   programs at museums, 29; on goals of
   National Gallery, 63; as museum board
   member, xxv–xxvi; as role model, 10;
   on women's rights, 19
Zayeddin, Fawzi, xxvi
Zayyaden, Fowzia, 18
Zeid, Fahrelnissa: accomplishments of,
   81–82; as artist/educator, 77, 111;
   dedication to the arts of, 89; influence
   of on Shoman, 50, 80; museum named
   after, xxxv
Al Zoubi, Amneh, 20
Zu'bi, Asma, 55, 103